Freakishly Effective Entrepreneur Success Secret

Discover Millionaire Self-Discipline Habits to Create an Unshakeable Business and Master the Money Makeover for Financial Freedom, Achieve Prosperity

Jeremy Napier

© **Copyright 2019 - All rights reserved.**

The content contained within this book may not be reproduced, duplicated or transmitted without direct written permission from the author or the publisher.

Under no circumstances will any blame or legal responsibility be held against the publisher, or author, for any damages, reparation, or monetary loss due to the information contained within this book. Either directly or indirectly.

<u>Legal Notice:</u>
This book is copyright protected. This book is only for personal use. You cannot amend, distribute, sell, use, quote or paraphrase any part, or the content within this book, without the consent of the author or publisher.

Disclaimer Notice:

Please note the information contained within this document is for educational and entertainment purposes only. All effort has been executed to present accurate, up to date, and reliable, complete information. No warranties of any kind are declared or implied. Readers acknowledge that the author is not engaging in the rendering of legal, financial, medical or professional advice. The content within this book has been derived from various sources. Please consult a licensed professional before attempting any techniques outlined in this book.

By reading this document, the reader agrees that under no circumstances is the author responsible for any losses, direct or indirect, which are incurred as a result of the use of information contained within this document, including, but not limited to, — errors, omissions, or inaccuracies.

Contents

Paycheck to Paycheck to Millionaire _____ 1

Introduction _____ 2

Chapter 1:
Mindset _____ 5

Chapter 2:
Stop Buying Lottery Tickets _____ 24

Chapter 3:
The Power of a Goal _____ 34

Chapter 4:
No Plan B, Only Plan A _____ 43

Chapter 5:
Life's not Fair _____ 49

Chapter 6:
You're Going to Die _____ 59

Chapter 7:
Never Be Satisfied _____ 69

Chapter 8:
Go Big or Go Home _____ 76

Chapter 9:
Positive Optimism _____ 87

Chapter 10:
Haters Criticism _____ 96

Chapter 11:
Never Tap Out _____ 103

Chapter 12:
Millionaire Success Hacks _____ 114

Chapter 13:
The Challenge_____ 128

How To _____ 133

Chapter 1:
Habits _____ 134

Chapter 2:
Start Your Day Right _____ 147

Chapter 3:
Life is Unfair, Get Over It _____ 156

Chapter 4:
Embrace the Hurdles in Life _____ 167

Chapter 5:
Uncomfortable Means Opportunity _____ 177

Chapter 6:
Easy Offers No Reward _____ 186

Chapter 7:
Judging A Book by Its Cover Will Be Your Downfall _____ 195

Chapter 8:
You Can't Conquer the World Alone _____ 206

Chapter 9:
The Power of Your Mind is Limitless _____ 216

Chapter 10:
Awaking the Giant when Defeated and Broken _____ 225

Chapter 11:
Never Ring the Bell _____ 233

Chapter 12:
Final Note _____ 244

2 IN 1 VALUE

FREAKISHLY EFFECTIVE ENTREPRENEUR SUCCESS SECRETS

Discover Millionaire Self-Discipline Habits to Create an Unshakeable Business and Master the Money Makeover for Financial Freedom,

JEREMY NAPIER

Paycheck to Paycheck to Millionaire

The Path to Wealth and Financial Freedom. Learn the Unshakeable Habits for Success and Prosperity

Introduction

To be successful, you need to achieve your goals, and to achieve the goals you set you need to have a positive mindset. Unfortunately, the failure to achieve set goals leaves many of us feeling disappointed and depressed which drives us to give up on the goals entirely. Success requires definite goals and the commitment and desire to realize the goals. Success cannot be achieved overnight; it is paramount that you know that it is a time-consuming process that requires hard work and patience to be successful.

To be among the few who succeed, you should know how to achieve your goals, and you must take the pursuit of success seriously. There are those who do not set goals at all but still hope to achieve the things they want- they certainly get some of the results they want but find most of their desires elusive because they do not have a plan. They pursue their goals by groping in the dark, which is frustrating, uncertain and tiring.

Paycheck to Paycheck to Millionaire

Success begins with finding a purpose, then defining and identifying specific goals to help you attain the purpose, and then mapping out a detailed action plan to guide and help you achieve the purpose.

Do you want to be successful in life? Do you want to achieve everything that you always wanted to? If your answers are yes, this book is exactly what you need right now! As you flip through the pages, you will find detailed insight on everything that you've ever wanted to know about being successful in life.

So, if you're really looking to make it big in life and achieve things that are practically impossible for others, give this book a try! It'll give you great insights on how to achieve and sustain success.

By following the insights in this book and going after your goals daily, you will develop and master the success elements you need to achieve your goals. Achieving your goals is not easy, and you will indeed be faced with some trying moments, however, through self-belief, positivity, and by following a clear action plan, you will have the commitment, focus, resilience and will to achieve everything you set out to do. Additionally, you will learn to apply the success tenets to overcome the inertia which often stifles goals even before you begin pursuing them.

You have probably heard this before, that success is all about the mindset –the person with the right mindset will get what he or she wants while those with a fickle mental attitude will almost always fail.

Jeremy Napier

Our thoughts determine whether we shall succeed at something or not; you basically have the power to decide what direction and how high your achievements are going to be.

Chapter 1:
Mindset

What is success to you?

Most people have different definitions of success, but they all boil down to how happy they are, how healthy they are and how much wealth they have. One way to be successful is to have a positive mindset. This means that you must believe that you are capable of the success that you desire and that you have beliefs that can support and sustain your success. It does not really matter how hard you work to obtain wealth; if you do not have positive beliefs about money, then wealth will always seem to be moving away from you.

Many people desire wealth but have negative beliefs about money. This is partly due to their subconscious mind. In order to understand this, you need to understand that your mind isn't just one unified clamp of cells that sits atop your shoulders. It has three main parts, the conscious mind, the subconscious mind, and the superconscious mind. The superconscious mind is sometimes referred to as the universal mind. It contains the collective knowledge of humanity and is the source of imagination and inspiration.

The subconscious mind can be likened to the operating system of a computer. It contains most of our programs and beliefs that direct how we behave, what we believe and is responsible for storing our habits and our memories. The conscious mind is the rational part of you that evaluates life and is always trying to solve problems. It's the part that is normally 'talking' in our heads (for example, when you are reading without vocalizing) and is always jumping from idea to idea. When you desire to change your life, it is easy to make the decision consciously, but this rarely sticks. It is only by bringing your subconscious mind on board that you can create lasting change.

The subconscious mind mostly contains ideas, memories, and beliefs that we acquire when we are children. This is because, at that stage, we had no way of knowing if what our elders told us was true or not, and we accepted their ideas without questioning. This is bad because we sometimes acquire negative beliefs from people who meant well but did not know any better. For example, if your parents believed and told you that they had always been poor and that getting money was hard, then unless you come to refute those beliefs, they will continue to be true to your life. What your subconscious believes normally becomes your reality.

The best thing about the subconscious mind is that it does not rationalize. If you come to change those beliefs in adulthood and believe for example, that you can become wealthy, the moment your subconscious accepts it, your reality will begin to alter to match your new beliefs. This, however, means that you must work hard at uprooting any negative beliefs that you may have about health, wealth and happiness and begin to actively install beliefs that are in line with the kind of life you desire. The best decision you can make for yourself is to take an active role in directing your life. This means you begin to analyze your life and the beliefs that you hold and begin disputing negative beliefs and installing new ones in line with who you want to be.

For many people, they begin to realize the negative beliefs they have when they find out what they want and begin to actively pursue it. When you discover your purpose, you begin to change how you think about your life. If you decide to pursue this purpose, normally it requires that you develop strong beliefs in yourself and begin to actively change your life so that the achievement of your dreams is possible. This change in perspective and priorities are sometimes so radical that people change who they are completely to become the kind of people who can achieve their dreams.

Anything Is Possible

It is not yet known what the full capabilities of a human being are. We use a very small percentage of our brain, and even the world's geniuses do not come close to utilizing half of their brain capacity. What this implies is that we are capable of a great deal more than we think we are. Normally the only limits we have are the ones we place on ourselves. As far as life is concerned, anything is possible.

Consider how Olympic records get broken time and time again, even though we always think we have reached the threshold of speed. Consider all the people who change their circumstances, rise above the obstacles they encounter and thrive even at times when change is considered impossible. What about all the companies that begin and succeed during economic depressions. What this implies is that you define what is impossible in your life. Whatever you decide is impossible, you will never go past it until you change what you believe.

Have A Purpose

We have talked about how having a purpose may propel you to make great changes in your life. Having a purpose is sometimes defined as having a 'why.' Your purpose is the product of your passions and your values. When you have a passion for something, it means you have a strong emotional drive towards pursuing and accomplishing that thing. Most of the time, the difference between the tasks you perform excellently at and the tasks that you are subpar at is how much passion you had towards the task. For example, a teacher who is passionate about teaching may go above what may be required of them to ensure that their students succeed while one without the passion may do the bare minimum

Your values are based on what you believe is important, particularly in terms of morals and beliefs. Examples of values include honesty, integrity, excellence, kindness, and freedom. Your values help clarify what you are willing to do and how you behave. For example, a person who values freedom may be more inclined towards self-employment opportunities while one who values honesty will be dissuaded from jobs that do not follow this value for example, stealing. You can very easily define your purpose if you take your passions and your values into account. There are many benefits of knowing your purpose and some of them are discussed below.

- Having a purpose clarifies your direction. Having a purpose may be likened to having a map of where you are going.

- Your purpose helps you maintain your focus on the goals you want to achieve.

- Having a purpose is the first step in creating a plan. Unless you know where you are going, you cannot create a plan to go there.

- Having a purpose helps in avoiding distractions. You are less likely to engage in harmful and useless behaviors when you have a purpose you are actively pursuing.

- A purpose is a remedy for confusion. Confusion stems from having a directionless life.

- A purpose is useful in living a life you enjoy. If you are following your passions, then you will enjoy the pursuit of your dreams.

- A purpose allows you to live a congruent life. A congruent life is one that is in alignment with what you value and what you believe.

- A purpose is useful in making day to day decisions as it allows you to distinguish between what is important and what isn't.

- Having a purpose helps you define your commitments and motivates you to act.

Why You Need a Life Purpose

A Purpose Is the Starting Point of The Life You Are Meant to Live

A life purpose is the first step to living the life that you are meant to live. Without a purpose, your life is basically an aimless unfocused pursuit of many unclear goals- you can live a life chasing goals which in the end turn out to be an illusion, something you do not want.

With a life purpose, you consciously pursue what you really want despite the challenges there may be, with the full knowledge and commitment to what you want to achieve in the long run. A purpose will lead to the right goals, an actionable plan and deliberate steps for a meaningful life.

A Clear Understanding of What Is Important

The point here is really about priority- a purpose helps you decipher what is important and what is not. Many times, we do not really know what is important and what is not because we do not have a clear understanding of what our purpose is. We do not know what we are really meant to do; therefore, we do not know how to prioritize our goals.

To Give Meaning to Life

Without a doubt, when you have a purpose, you have the 'why' for your life- you have the meaning of life. Purpose gives your life a clear direction and meaning which means that you will achieve more as compared to running around without a purpose. A life with meaning is a happier and healthier life with better odds of success.

Drive and Focus

A purpose is a passion. When you are on a journey to achieve a purpose, you will be filled with enthusiasm and passion for attaining it. With passion, you get an inextinguishable drive and focus on staying on course and jumping any hurdles that get in the way of achieving your life purpose. Purpose boosts performance and energy physically and mentally to pursue your goals and ultimately realize your vision.

Success

Success is about doing the right thing to achieve what you want. What better guide to success than a clear purpose! Instead of seeking success unto itself, find your purpose and use it to succeed—direct your energy to do what you like and make success a reality by doing what makes you happy. Discovering your true purpose is the easiest and surest way to success.

A purpose is a powerful part of our being, and once you identify what your purpose is, nothing can really stop you from achieving any height of success. Therefore, before you begin setting any goals, you need to find out what your purpose is in life because by pursuing what you are passionate about your chances of success are raised exponentially. If you are not happy with what you are doing or are feeling empty and aimless with your goals, it is probable that you have not pinpointed what your purpose truly is.

How to Discover Your Purpose?

Like we have discussed above, your purpose should be something that you are interested in and are enthused about. It is very difficult to commit to a purpose which you do not like. Here is a short process which you can use to find your purpose

Interrogate Your Abilities and Strengths

We innately have a deep purpose in us which we can and should discover. All you need to do it to discover what it is that you are meant to do and achieve, and you will have discovered your purpose. People have different purposes based on interests and abilities- you only must discover where your strengths are. That is why in the creation of wealth, for example, there are varied ways of how people make money- artists, lawyers, doctors, sportsmen, etc.

In other words, the result is success money wise; however, the means of getting there is really a purpose which it either a talent skill, interest, etc. Ask yourself the following questions as you explore your abilities and strengths- what you love doing and what comes to you effortlessly. Your purpose should be something that makes you happy and does not require you to struggle to do.

Identify Your Top Expressed Qualities and How You Enjoy Expressing Them

You already know that you are born with your purpose which is lying latently awaiting activation to help you realize your vision and to help you succeed. Therefore, in finding your purpose, you should identify the top qualities you possess, your strengths, and how you most enjoy using or express them. In your top qualities or strengths lies your life purpose, and in how you best express them lies the foundation on which to base your goals and vision.

Create Purpose Mantra

A purpose mantra is basically a personal statement to describe your vision to always remind you of what you are meant to achieve. Mantras are very powerful tools that will not only remind you of your target but will also ensure that you have a positive mindset to believe and commit to your goals and purpose.

Follow Your Instincts

There is no more accurate and reliable guide in whatever you do than your instinct. Your inner guide is always correct and is something that you must consult and listen to always as you identify and commit to purpose. It will navigate the path to your purpose and help you work through your goals to get you there. Your inner voice will plot a reliable map for you to follow to reach your destination successfully.

How to Have A Mindset for Success

It is now quite clear that you need to have a positive mindset in order to be successful. You may now ask what can be considered a positive mindset. Generally, we can consider two main types of mindsets. People normally have either one in different categories of their life, and it determines how successful they are.

There is a growth mindset and a fixed mindset. A growth mindset is a future-oriented mindset while a fixed mindset is past-oriented. A person with a growth mindset believes that their lives can change, that they can go after the things they desire and that they can grow, learn and adapt. On the other hand, a person with a fixed mindset does not believe that they can change, learn, grow or adapt. In order to achieve success, you must have a growth mindset.

Develop A Positive Mindset

Unwavering commitment requires a positive mindset more than anything else, yet it remains one of the most challenging habits to master. In fact, a lack of the right mindset is the number one reason why many of us will not achieve our goals. A positive mindset will help you to pursue your goals relentlessly- it gives you the ability to get back on track and to learn from failures. To be successful, you must believe that you can succeed.

How to Create A Positive Mindset?

Once we know our life's purpose, we can them begin to form and nurture a positive mindset to help us achieve the goals we set to reach our purpose. The power of positive thinking is incredible; if you hope for the best and look forward to good times, then you will have a happier, less stressful and successful life.

Positive thinking is a mental state where one expects to get favorable outcomes in whatever they do. Positive thinking therefore means that you actively train your mind to bear creative thoughts that transform energy into reality. We are what we think- by allowing negative thoughts and fears to rule your mind, you are destined to be captive to the ensuing pressures.

The first thing you must do to attain positive thoughts is to stop dwelling on your failures and put more emphasis on your successes. Highlight and concentrate on your accomplishments at work and use the things that did not turn out as expected purely as lessons for future endeavors. Failures are not supposed to weigh you down; they are supposed to make you better and stronger; they are lessons or reference points but not condemnation.

Studies and research have proved that those who practice positive thinking are more successful at goal setting. Achieving goals and realizing our life's purpose is not possible without the right mental attitude to align our abilities and focus on what we set out to do. A positive mindset will give you direction and purpose. Unfortunately, many of us have trouble tuning and focusing our minds to help us reach our purpose. A positive mindset will give you the best chance of reaching your goals.

Goal setting and success without a positive mindset and the resultant drive to achieve your goals leads to failure, and that is why many of us never achieve what we set out to do. It is because we do not know or omit to cultivate a positive mindset required to chase our goals successfully. If you do not develop a positive mindset you will struggle to overcome the challenges of pursuing your goals. A positive mindset is what will keep you going by enabling you to concentrate on the positives, however difficult things get, and will help you to pursue and visualize your goals for success.

Having a positive mindset for success begins with changing your environment to reflect your purpose and vision- it is impossible to sustain a positive mindset in a negative environment. You start by improving your immediate physical surrounding. So, how do you become a positive thinker?

The only way to be successful at positive thinking is to be able to tell what a negative thought is and to work at keeping them at bay. Examples of negativity or negative thoughts are:

- If you find yourself sieving out positive aspects of a situation and dwelling on the negative. For example, you are complimented at work for completing an assignment ahead of time then instead of enjoying the compliment; you instead embark on thinking of ways to even finish your assignments faster than you did.

- You take the blame for everything bad that happens. When a problem arises, you are quick to blame yourself even for things you ought not to beat yourself over.

- Living in fear of a catastrophe by always expecting the worst to come your way. You get soiled by a car splashing rainwater on the road, and you automatically decide that your day is doomed. You condemn yourself to have a bad day.

- You are a prisoner of perfection. Nothing is worth your while unless it is perfect and things in your world are either bad or good with nothing in between.

How to Focus Positivity in Your Mind?

Positive People
Start your shift to a positive mindset with the people around you get rid of negative who will be toxic to your plans and purpose and replace them with like-minded people who understand what you are working at and will advise, encourage and support you. Replace negative

people with those who will help you with your weaknesses and complement your strengths.

Positive Surroundings

Since mindset is about thoughts, you want to be in a surrounding which will conjure positive thoughts and feelings to enable a positive mindset that will ensure that you are mentally relaxed, creative and high performing to realize your vision. Your surroundings should inspire and motivate you.

Clean up your space and get rid of clutter, light up your space with natural lighting to boost brain function, and have vision boards to remind you of your goals and what you need to do.

Positive Thoughts

Your mind is the most important tool in the journey to success and wealth creation, and if your mind is not tuned for success, you cannot achieve any of your goals. A positive mindset requires positive thoughts which will spawn positive habits which lead to actions aligned to pursuing the goals you set and creates a goal oriented subconscious to imprint your purpose and vision in your thoughts.

Distinguish the negative aspects of your thinking and areas of your job that need changing. Identify the poisonous areas and work towards changing them; begin being more hopeful and optimistic.

Evaluate your thoughts by having a periodical assessment of your mindset throughout your workday. If you discover your mind is harboring negative thoughts, redirect your thought to more positive things.

Take it easy. Do not be too uptight or sad to allow yourself moments of joy. You need to laugh even more during and about the difficult things you may be facing. Laughter reduces stress.

Be a self-motivator by always encouraging yourself. Look at the positive side of everything and always be optimistic.

Positive habits are integral to attaining goals- they keep you on track and suppress negative ways. Develop positive habits is easy and all it requires is consistency. Creating a success mindset requires you to be repetitive and consistent with positive mindset habits. Remember, your thoughts create the things you want and the person you will be.

Developing a positive mindset is critical for success because, without a success mindset, you cannot take the steps required to achieve your goals especially when things become challenging. Developing a positive mindset is not something that can be done overnight; it takes time, practice and habituation to master. Remember that you are introducing into your life something that is completely alien.

Commitment and persistence are really the fuel that will keep you pursuing your goals and are integral for success. By developing an unrelenting commitment to achieving a goal, any challenges, obstacles and even failures that you meet along the way can easily be overcome. The belief and commitment you have for your life purpose should constantly feed and ignite in you the desire to succeed.

Besides the characteristics of a growth mindset mentioned above, there are other components of a growth mindset that increase your chances of attaining success. These are:

Having A Plan

Human beings are goal oriented. We find fulfillment by overcoming challenges and adapting. Whenever we are rudderless, we have a tendency towards depression and confusion, but when we are actively planning and executing on our goals, we find joy and fulfillment. Self-actualization is the highest need in Maslow's hierarchy of needs. Self-actualization refers to the fulfillment of the potential a person has.

According to Maslow, self-actualization is a vital motivator after the motivation to fulfill one's physiological needs (food, clothing, shelter, love, and belonging). Some theories of human development also find that contentment in old age comes as a result of looking back at your life and finding that you have made significant life accomplishments.

Having Good Relationships

Human beings are social creatures. When it comes to becoming rich, there are two main ways of gaining wealth: providing a service that solves people's problems or providing art. The wealth you desire is in the hands of other people and the methods are the main ways to obtain it. Relationships are important because we are the sum of the people we stay around. When you have a growth mindset, it is important to stay around people who have the same view of life as you so that you may grow together.

Having Perseverance

A person with a fixed mindset focuses on the failure, a person with a growth mindset focusses on the process, and the lessons learned. Life is defined by what you do just as much as it is determined by how well you persevere. The more challenges you face and overcome in the course of attaining your dreams, the more fulfilled you will be. In life, there is no such thing as smooth sailing. In fact, the most absolute thing about life is that it is always changing. You must learn to adapt to the new changes if you desire to grow.

Perseverance is witnessed before a business begins its operations and throughout the course of its operations. We should not be afraid of facing challenges or failing rather we should be afraid of remaining the same. This is because it means you are not really growing. Positive relationships are vital when it comes to perseverance. You need people who will keep cheering you on as you go through life's speed bumps. Don't forget to be your own biggest cheerleader too.

The Willingness to Learn

They say there is nothing new under the sun. If you have an idea you wish to implement in order to be successful and achieve wealth, there is probably someone out there who had a similar idea. There are two kinds of people generally, those who learn from their mistakes and those who learn from the mistakes of others.

We live in a digital era which reduces our planet to a digital village. You have two choices, you can go through the long way of learning, or you can fast track yourself and therefore fail smarter and better. Learning does not guarantee that you will not make any mistakes, it just ensures that you avoid those mistakes that you can.

How to Make Decisions to Help You Achieve Your Goals?

In order to achieve success, you need to make just one decision, to go after what it is that you desire. This is only possible if you know that which you desire (you have a purpose) and then creating an actionable plan and following it through so that you make your dreams a reality. The best way to make sure that you can achieve your goals is to write them down. If you consistently focus on your goals, you will be able to start making progress on your dreams which brings you closer to success.

If you desire to be successful in your life, you will need to have a positive mindset. Believe that what you desire is possible for you. We live in a limitless universe that rewards hard work and focused attention. All you must do is to decide once and for all. Find your purpose, make actionable plans, execute, review and repeat until you accomplish what you desire.

You have a choice when it comes to your mindsets and belief. The next time a problem arises in your time, stop and analyze your first reactions. Are they characteristic of a growth mindset or a fixed mindset? always Take responsibility for your own mindset and decide today to have a positive mindset.

Chapter 2:
Stop Buying Lottery Tickets

In the pursuit of wealth, there is a certain appeal to shortcuts. Take a lottery ticket for example, while it may cost you just a little money, you can win millions. However, it is also an easy way of losing money. When you are broke or short of funds, it is easy to fantasize that you will be a winner (and you can), but there is a reason this is a fantasy.

First, the odds are not in your favor. The odds get lower and lower depending on the number of digits you must pick and the range of these digits. Compounded by the fact that you may have to participate severally leading to spending more money you don't have to buy more lottery tickets and it really makes no sense why you would participate in the lottery.

Lottery tickets can also be any silver bullets you think could get you to those riches faster. From gambling to get rich quick schemes, there is a whole industry that preys on individuals who desire money now. They gain more from you than you do from them.

You May Ask, Then What Can I Do?

The best and safest bet you have is to be prepared to do actual work. You must pick one plan that you think will work and then you must focus on it until it succeeds or until experience proves that it won't in which case you discard it. If you desire success, stop spending your hard-earned money on fantasies and get to work.

The Foundation of Success Is Hard Work

Anyone who desires success must be ready to pay the price for it and many times the price is simply to work hard. Working hard for success may be defined as the diligence to pursue and complete tasks geared towards achieving a goal or set of goals which will enable the attainment of success. We live in an era that may not value hard work as much as it values smart work. Smart work means analyzing the tasks that you are meant to do and concentrating on the tasks that move you forward the most.

A lot of people work hard every day, but they work on the mundane, monotonous tasks rather than giving priority to the tasks that have the most impact. While you will still work hard, you will be selective about where you put your effort. All references to hard work shall, therefore, refer to diligent, focused, smart work. When working hard, there are some important things you need to do.

It is important that you dream big and you set goals. It is on these goals that you work hard. It is useless to commit to toiling every day with no end goal in mind. In fact, it is impossible to separate important work from unimportant work if you do not have criteria from which to judge your tasks. When you have goals, you must break them down into daily, and weekly action plans. This process of breaking down goals involves analyzing what tasks will get you ahead faster and assigning them to yourself daily. Work hard comes in by ensuring that you stick to this plan no matter what. It is vital that you decide, and you commit to it.

When you have a goal, it is not deciding that pushes you to work on your goal but the commitment to the result. You must commit to the plan you have and to the daily actions you have decided are important. If you have decided to start a business and you determine that it's important that you read about business management and financial management every day, it is your commitment to read every day that will improve your knowledge. After all, many people decide on goals every New Year's Day, but very few people stay committed to the decision. Commitment also increases your endurance when things go wrong because you refuse to be defeated. In the end, it's the ones who commit that succeed

If you want to be successful, you must be ready to gain experience. Some people get caught in a learning trap. They want to be perfect before they start. They spend days planning, reading and generally trying to prevent any problems they think they will encounter that they never actually go out and gain experience. While it is not bad to want to be ready, the future is uncertain, and at some point, you will have to do the actual work. Remind yourself that obstacles are inevitable, but they are not fatal. You must be ready to fail a few times in the process of becoming better. You may have as much theoretical knowledge as you desire, but it will never be worth more than experience.

You need to be willing to network. Go out and meet people who are working in the same field as you. If you are brave, you can even visit those that are against your ideas. Those in your line will share with you what they know and what they have done that has worked while those against your ideas will push you to think of ways to expand your brand so that they too may benefit. Keep in mind, however, that you can't please everyone.

In the process of networking, you will be able to make healthy relationships with different people. You can learn all you wish to learn and be an expert in your field but remember the money you want is with other people. When you are out there making meaningful connections, you increase your chances of success compared to when you stay in isolation.

Importance of Hard Work

Hard work leads to results which serve as a basis for evaluation. When you begin to work hard towards a goal, you begin to start making progress. In the process of executing your plans, you may encounter stumbling blocks, and you may fail a few times. With the right mindset, you can transform these failures into teachable moments. Look for the lesson to be learned from the failure and then course correct so that you increase your chances of success. If you are not making progress, then you have no way of knowing what parts of your plan work and what parts don't.

Hard work creates opportunities. Deliberate, consistent action towards your goal allows you to gain experience which you can share particularly with those of like mind. In this process, you get opportunities to learn and to meet people for example partners, investors and customers. People are normally very willing to help, but they can't help you if you are seated on your couch doing nothing. You can take your idea to someone who is doing it on a larger scale, and they may be willing to help you, but only if they see that you have potential, you know what you are doing and that you are hard working. You don't need to be an expert to approach the pros, but don't expect that they will have the time to teach you everything

Working hard teaches you useful values. Hard work is a good value to learn, but you can also learn time management, consistency, persistence, excellence, etc. These values are useful in day to day life, and they affect how people view you. If you are trying to create a brand, for example, a business, these values are also reflected in your brand, and if they are good, they will attract people. Some people find that they don't have to spend a lot on marketing themselves because their good values market themselves through word of mouth. After all, people love talking about good things.

Focus on What You Can Control

You cannot control life. You may work as hard as you desire, but the outcomes are never in your hands. You should strive to focus on what you can control and many times it is your attitude and your actions. You control your actions by deliberately doing things that move you towards your goals. You control your attitude by deciding your mindset. You should always strive to have a positive mindset. A positive mindset means that you have positive expectations towards your future and that you react positively to all people and situations. A positive reaction normally involves choosing to take responsibility and looking for ways to solve the problems that arise instead of complaining.

Develop Self-Discipline

Hard work teaches you discipline. By consistently working on your goals, you train yourself to stick to the plan. You won't always feel like it, but if you have committed to it, then you must do it. This discipline will eventually seep into other areas of your life. Self-discipline is a very important quality to have if you desire success. This is because your goals are yours and no one will push you to go after them. There are some areas that will require your hard work and discipline if you desire success and they are elaborated below.

You need to have the discipline to manage your time effectively. We all have twenty-four hours in a day, yet you always find people who seem to do more with their day than others. By managing your time, you can dedicate specific amounts of time to the things that you want to accomplish. Time management will also allow you to allocate time to leisure and your relationships. It has the added advantage of allowing you to enjoy that time because you are not worried about unfinished work and unmet deadlines. If you wish to eliminate worry and stress in your life when it comes to work, it is mandatory that you learn how to utilize your time effectively

If you want to produce your best work, you must be ready to develop yourself. Self-development requires self-discipline because it rarely profits anyone but yourself. Furthermore, the process of self-development never ends. You develop yourself through continuous learning. Read books on how to change your outlook, the habits of successful people and how to be a better person.

Besides reading books, it is important to apply what you learn in your life. Install new habits that make you better. A word of caution though, books are written by individuals and they talk about what worked for them. However, no method is one-size-fits-all. If you try something and it does not work, be willing to discard it. In this way, you implement methods that help improve you, and you don't overburden yourself with things that don't work.

Paycheck to Paycheck to Millionaire

Discipline is necessary for financial management. If you desire to be wealthy, you need to leverage your resources and your cash flow so that they can earn for you. This does not necessarily mean that you need to go to school and learn finance. There are many books and seminars that are geared towards teaching individuals to manage their own finances. You can even hire a personal coach to train you. There are, however, some principles that are universal that you should obey. These include:

- Your expenses should never exceed your income. When your expenses exceed what you are earning, you begin to accumulate debt which reduces how much usable income you have and thus begins a vicious cycle.

- You should always save. It is advisable that you save before you begin to spend not save whatever remains.

- Minimize your expenses whenever possible so that you can save. Prioritize on essentials and reward yourself with luxuries and non-essentials.

- Invest your money. When you invest, you can compound your money through interest, therefore making your money earn for you.

- Track your money. This is the best way to be able to identify where your money is going and how you can use it better

- Don't keep all your eggs in one basket. When it comes to investments, diversify your portfolio so that you do not lose all your money if an investment does not work out as expected.

There are many ways to acquire riches. Some are what we call silver bullets; they are shortcuts that promise you that you can get money without having to do any actual work. The main problem is that these methods favor very few people. The other problem is about self-actualization. We value what we work hard for more than what we get for free or what we get for no work. If you desire lasting riches and accomplishment, stop looking for the next best solution to make you money fast. Get creative. Think of a plan that might work, execute it and tackle any challenges you face in order to get success. If you pair this advice with the following pointers, you are well on your way to success.

- Learn the difference between hard work and smart work.

- Learn financial management.

- Learn to be self-disciplined

What silver bullets have you been using in your life trying to get wealth faster? Ask around for the number of people who have gained significant success using those methods. You may be surprised how few they are.

Paycheck to Paycheck to Millionaire

The lottery ticket or any other silver bullet are the irrefutable items that most of us buy in abundance that is a complete waste of money. If you are guilty of investing too much of your time and money on lottery tickets you need to stop, channel that effort and financial investment into something tangible and more pragmatic in order to reach 100% of your true potential.

Now, what plan have you been putting off that you know might work? Start today. You will be surprised where you will be a year from now if you are consistent.

Chapter 3:
The Power of a Goal

A goal is a desired vision and outcome that a person or an organization visualizes, plans for, and commits to achieving. For many people, the only goals they set in their lives are New Year's resolutions which are often discarded by January 15th. If you were to analyses some of the most successful people, however, they will all tell you that their success came as a result of having goals that they actively worked towards. A goal is an external representation of the desires a person has. Setting goals are not hard, but the success that follows executed goals is amazing. Many times, goals are stated in terms of the end results that one desires, for example, one can have a goal to lose weight, to travel, to get a certain result in school or even to purchase an object like a laptop

There are mainly two types of goals, task-based goals, and performance-based goals. A task-based goal is one that focuses on the activities that a person wants to perform or wants to be able to perform at the end of a specified amount of time. Performance-based goals on the other hand focus or what a person desires to achieve at the end of the goal.

It is often better to set task-based goals rather than performance-based goals. This is because you have control over what actions you take, but most of the time, your performance is not something you can control. This is normally the main reason why many New Year resolutions fail. Those who set resolutions to lose weight, for example, find that they have no control over how fast they can shed off the weight. Those who, however, set goals to exercise a certain number of times a week can easily measure if they are failing at their task or not and therefore, they are better able to stick to their goals.

Why You Should Set Goals

You cannot get to any destination if you do not know where it is. Let's say you desire to visit a national park a few states away. This is your goal. When you know where you want to go, you can now buy the correct map, pack the things you need for the trip, set aside the money you think will allow you to make this trip and even organize how you will get to the destination. All these steps arise as a result of knowing your destination. That is the main importance of setting a goal; it clarifies what you will need to do and become in order to achieve your dreams.

There are resources out there that will give you the information you need on how you can set your goals. However, there are a few important things you need to consider when setting your goals.

Your goals should be balanced. You need to set goals that grow and evolve your life completely, not just career or health goals. When people focus on growing aspects of their lives and ignore others, they often find that they end up not being as happy as they would like when they achieve their goals. Take an example of a wealthy lawyer or CEO who went after his career goals at the expense of his wealth and his relationships.

While he may achieve the wealth and career success he desired, he may have no close family or friends to celebrate with and spend his wealth on, or he may be sick and need to channel most of his wealth into medical bills. When you create goals in the categories of your life that are important to you, you can enjoy your life more. In fact, one of the most common regrets of the people on their death beds is that they worked too hard at the expense of their health and relationships. The main categories you can consider when setting your goals are:

- Health and wellbeing
- Family and relationships
- Career and work
- Money and material possessions
- Creativity and experiences

You also need to define your goals and why you want them. Defining your goals is useful in clarifying what it is that you want. When you add why it is that you want this goal, you are better able to distinguish between goals that are worthwhile from those that aren't. The best way to define your goals is by writing them down. You are better able to analyze your goals when they are written down.

This process of writing your goals down allows for reflection and introspection which is very important. It is not uncommon for people to write down their goals and to realize that they are not realistic, that they will not lead to the wealth and success they desire or that they really aren't their goals but other people's visions they took on as their own. Your goals should always be in line with your purpose, your vision and your mission in life.

Break down your goals into actionable plans. When you have your goals written down, you are now able to break them down into steps that you can follow. How do you eat an elephant? One bite at a time. It does not really matter how big your goals are. They just need to be measurable and attainable. In order to make an actionable plan, decide how you will know when your goal is achieved. Then break down how you can get to this point by figuring out your yearly, monthly and weekly milestones. Once you know what you desire to do on a weekly basis, then you can set up daily habits and routines that will support you in attaining your goal. The reason you set daily habits is that they allow you to make daily progress towards your goal and they give you something to commit to.

Set deadlines, track your progress and schedule your time. When you have an end goal in mind, you should also decide on a reasonable deadline. This will help you understand and define your weekly, monthly and yearly milestones. Also setting deadlines allows you to divide your goals into short term goals and long-term goals. Once you know what these are, you can now schedule your time.

Some people do this by deciding a minimum number of hours they wish to work on their goals each week, and some decide to set daily time blocks for their goals. This allows you to come up with routines you can follow daily and weekly so that you meet your milestones. You can only track what you can measure and having this time blocks is a very good way to track your progress. When you can see how far you have come from, you become motivated to keep the momentum and persevere with your goals.

Having goals sometimes requires you to tailor your environment so that it works for you. For example, if you decide that you want to be working on a certain project at a particular time every day, you can find a quiet place to be working from every day and even remove any distractions in that environment so that you work effectively. You can also anticipate your physical needs so that you are always ready for that time. If it is after lunch, for example, you can ensure that you always eat beforehand, you can switch your phone off to reduce distractions, and you can even ask that you are not disturbed during that time as you need to focus. Your environment can assist you in achieving your dreams, or it can lead to senseless distractions which later lead to incomplete milestones.

Importance of Goals

As was mentioned earlier, having a goal is like having a map. Goals give you a sense of direction. They allow you to know what it is that you are required to do and why, so that you can achieve your dreams. Besides this reason, there are other benefits of having goals and the main ones are discussed below.

Goals direct your focus. Many people aimlessly go through life reacting to life's circumstances and never seeing what they can really become. When you have a goal, you can know what is important and what isn't and therefore you are able to be focused. For example, if you decide that your goal is to work several hours a day on creating a business with a friend, you will not spend your time sitting in front of the television when you know that that time can be better spent researching and reading about how to make that business work. You will focus on activities that build your goals.

Goals help in decision making. When you have a goal, you are clear on what it is that you want out of your life. Someone with a goal to live healthy will have an easier time saying no to requests by friends to go out and eat unhealthy foods. When you have decided to take several steps towards your goal, you take a lot of the willpower struggle out of your decision-making process. You have to make many decisions throughout the day, and when you have clear goals, you are working towards, some decisions become easier to make as you can just ask yourself if the decision you are making is in line with your goals or not

Goals can be a substitute for motivation. We do not always feel like doing the things we know we ought to do. Many of the times, the decisions that we must make and the habits we must keep in order to attain our goals won't feel good now. No one feels like exercising all the time, and no one wants to choose reading a business management book over the hot new thriller every day. However, when you have set a goal to be healthy, you will be reminded that you are choosing the vegetables and you are reading that business book for the sake of achieving your goal. Review your goals and your milestones daily and you will find it becomes easier and easier to make the hard choice for the sake of your goals even when there is no motivation

Having goals allows you to prioritize your life. When you have goals you are working towards, you are better able to prioritize your actions so that you are productive. As we said earlier, the tasks required in order to achieve your goals don't always feel good. However, when you know why you are doing them, it is easier to make the right decisions. When organizing your day, week or month, you can very easily prioritize the tasks that are important in the achievement of your dreams above those that are just for enjoyment. This does not mean that you don't get to do enjoyable things anymore, but that you can start out your day with the tasks you have to do and have less guilt when you have time to relax and enjoy your day

Goals allow you to build momentum. According to Newton's law of inertia, an object will remain stationary unless acted upon by an unbalanced force. This law can be applied to life and for the pursuit of success. When you have no goals, you may be an object at rest. You will not make any progress towards any dreams you have until you set goals. Your goals are the unbalanced force that will force you to start making progress. Once you are working on your goals, you begin to move towards them, and you will begin to gain momentum. When you begin to see progress, you will not want to stop what you are doing because you will want to see how much more progress you can make. Other benefits of goals include:

- Goals give you hope and confidence that you can achieve what you desire.

- Goals help in beating the habit of procrastination.

- Goals lead you towards self-mastery and the fulfillment of your potential.

- Goals clarify what it is that you really want in your life.

- Goals teach you how to discipline and regulate yourself.

- Goals help in building positive habits.

- Goals help in improving your life as progress in one area encourages progress in other areas.

If you desire to make any worthwhile progress in your life, it is important that you define your goals in this area and come up with actionable steps you can take to achieve them. Success never happens by accident, and you must be deliberate in your life so that you can be successful. The first step is to set your goals. They will give you a sense of focus and direction that will increase your chances of success. Be ready to become the kind of person that can achieve that goal by taking deliberate action.

What do you want to happen in your life? Write it down in a task-oriented manner and break it down so that you can understand what you need to do to achieve it.

Chapter 4:
No Plan B, Only Plan A

Many people grow up knowing that it is important to have a backup plan. Some people use the advice to not put all their eggs in one basket as an excuse to come up with a backup plan, but new research in psychology and motivation is proving that this may not be the best advice when it comes to goal setting. The main reason for this is because it entertains the idea that you may fail. It allows for this possibility, and therefore it increases your chances of failure. There are many reasons why it is always better to just focus on one plan, and we shall elaborate on some of them here

It increases your focus. Imagine you have a plan to start a business. You, however, are not sure if your business is going to succeed, so you decide to come up with a backup plan just in case. What happens is that you must set up the time to plan for plan B as well as for plan A. This means that you divert part of the attention you would have given to your main plan to this other plan. This is a recipe for disaster because if there is someone else who has the same idea as you do, they will probably start it in a much shorter time than you will, and they will probably be focusing on it more, therefore, increasing their chances of success when compared to you. You are better off working on one plan, executing it then starting the other one later if you still wish to when you can give it all your attention

It increases motivation. A lot of the studies pertaining to why we shouldn't have a plan B always find that those who have a backup plan have less motivation to work on their goals than if they had just one plan. This can easily be explained using a classroom situation. If there are two students in a classroom, one who is from a poor family and who understands that education may be their only way out of poverty and another who is from a rich family and who knows that they will inherit a lot of money as soon as they finish their schoolwork and all they need to do is to get their diploma, who do you think will be more motivated to work hard in school?

The former student, by sheer virtue of having fewer options, will most probably (not always) work harder. Similarly, when you know that you have other options in case the one you are working on fails, you will not have that inner drive and urgency to work on your 'only' option and, therefore you will be less motivated to work hard.

It leads to more disciplined decision making. When you know that the plan you are working on is the only one you have, you are very careful when you make decisions that may affect that plan. You will be less inclined to take unnecessary risks that may lead to failure compared to someone else who knows that failure is not as fatal. You will analyze all the ways a certain opportunity could affect your plan both negatively and positively and pick the option that has the highest chances of succeeding. This discipline is what increases your chance of success.

It increases your willpower. Whenever you decide, you cut off all other options and decide to go in one direction. This means that you do not have to decide what it is that you will be working on at that time, and to make decisions pertaining to two plans when you should be dealing with, just one. This is important for willpower because your ability to make good decisions deteriorates as you make more and more decisions during the day. This is what is referred to as decision fatigue.

When you must make decisions about two plans instead of one, you are very likely to begin taking shortcuts so that you can get over the decision-making process. This can be done by making impulsive decisions or choosing inactivity altogether. If you desire to make the best decisions pertaining to your goals, you are better off working on one at a time

It reduces distractions. Much as we would like to believe that we can multitask, the human brain is best suited to work on one task at a time. When you have two plans, you are inclined to give them equal weight as either one of them could succeed. This means that if you come up with an idea that may work for plan B while working on plan A, you will be inclined to take time and think about it or to at least write it down. You will be pondering on the best way to ensure that they work, meaning you will need to do research on both and find time for both.

Compared to a person who has a singular plan they are executing, you will face more distractions, and you will have to be much disciplined in order to prevent one plan from taking up the time of another. Ditch the distraction of plan B and do one thing at a time and you will find that you make more progress and at a much faster rate

It reduces over analysis and second-guessing. The best example of this would be to compare two types of examinations. There are examinations that have open-ended questions, and there are multiple choice exams. In open-ended examinations, you must come up with a singular answer to the question. However, in multiple choice questions, you often find students second-guessing themselves. Sometimes when you look at the answers, you get that gut feeling of which answer is correct.

After analyzing the other answers offered, you begin to doubt if you really were correct and sometimes you choose a different answer only to later find out that your first instinct was the correct one. While it may seem better to have options, it would have been much better if you had just stuck to your original plan. This holds true when you have more than one plan. It is better to have just one option.

It increases your chances of success. This is true when you look at it from the perspective of your subconscious mind. The subconscious mind manifests your dominant thoughts. If you have a plan B, what you are telling yourself is that you don't think that your first plan will work. While it is quite okay to be afraid and everyone experiences that fear of failure at some point, when you give in to your fear and actually create a second plan, you send a message to yourself that you don't believe that your plan A will work. This will lead to your subconscious mind manifesting the failure you fear. When you ignore the doubt and keep working on your plan, you may fail, but it will not be as a result of a self-fulfilling prophecy. Feel the fear but follow through with your plan anyway and your subconscious mind will lead you to success. Often it is not the realists that succeed in life but the optimists

It makes you accountable for failure. A plan B may also be referred to as an emotional safety net or an escape route. As we mentioned earlier, everyone has that fear of failure. Those who create backup plans, however, forget that sometimes failure is actually a very good motivator. When you fail, you are inclined to analyze what it is that you did wrong and correct it so that you reduce the chances of failing in that way again. However, when you have a plan B, you are refusing to take accountability for any mistakes you may make that can lead to failure. Instead, you may choose to ditch the whole plan and find another one.

Such an attitude normally creates a habit of quitting and leads to very few accomplishments because there are very few things that become a complete success after the first attempt. Failure does not mean that you will not succeed, it just means that you need to review the plan and try again.

The worst thing you can do in the pursuit of your dreams, besides not setting actionable goals would be to give yourself permission to fail. This is what you are doing when you set a plan B. When you set your plan B you are doubting your first instinct you had to pursue plan A and setting an escape plan 'Just in case.' You are, therefore, more likely to fail because of this self-fulfilling prophecy and because of how the subconscious mind works. If you are not ready to go all in on your plan, ditch it and make plan B your plan A but do not let fear of failure and doubts rob you the opportunity to see what you can truly become.

Do you have a plan B? Why do you think your plan A will not work? What can you do to increase your chances of your plan A working? Focus on what you can do to make your plan A work and stop diverting your time and energy into two plans. This will just increase your chances of success.

Chapter 5:
Life's not Fair

Life is not fair, neither is it unfair. It just is. We can accept life as it comes, or we can keep fighting people and circumstances which will only result in frustration and discontentment. It is part of human nature to seek justice and fairness. In fact, when something unfair happens to us, the amygdala, and the primitive part of our brain that results in a fight or flight response is triggered. It results in fear or anger, therefore explaining why we feel these emotions whenever we witness unfair occurrences. It triggers such strong physical and emotional reactions that if one is not conscious, it may lead to actions that you may regret later.

Humans have developed a cortex (the thinking brain) around the amygdala, which should assist in thinking through our reactions before we respond. Neurologically, the thinking brain kicks in a few seconds after the amygdala. Therefore, we should not be too fast to respond with the initial emotions felt but should take time to think through the emotions and come up with a logical course of action.

Generally, people respond to unfairness in three significant ways, either they try to control everything, or they worry excessively about everything or they walk the middle path. Worrying is not bad, but excessive worry or rumination normally drains your energy, increases your anxiety and makes you feel helpless because your focus is on the problem leading to inaction.

On the other hand, control freaks try to control every aspect of the situation micromanaging everyone and everything. This is futile because you cannot control everything. The middle path is the best way whereby worry is your initial reaction, but you follow it up with brainstorming for a solution and then acting in this direction.

Some Things Are Out of Your Control

Much as we would like to believe that we are in control, there are very many things that are out of our control. Generally, the only things we have control over are our actions and our attitudes. Your attitude is a result of your perception. People do not like to feel helpless in situations, and this often results in coping mechanisms to manage the feeling of helplessness. Some of these coping mechanisms are:

- Complaining. This is a very common coping mechanism and is normally used when the person who feels like they have been wronged can't think of a way of solving the problem and therefore looks for reassurance and sometimes pity from others.

- Using drugs. While some people take drugs for recreation purposes, others use them to deal with stress, and to numb emotions, they do not want to feel.

- Binging. From over-eating to over-consumption of media (TV, Social media and books) some people try to cope with stress through overconsumption rather than taking decisive action.

- Blaming and projecting. This is whereby someone decides to give the responsibility of the stress to someone else and to judge them as the guilty party.

- Using excuses. Some people always try to explain away their mistakes as a way of alleviating guilt or blame. It is a way of rationalizing your decisions after you have done them.

While these coping mechanisms may relieve the feeling for some time, they are useless when it comes to solving the problem. That is why some habits are repeated rather than looking for solutions that would solve the problem once and for all. How a person reacts to a problem may be indicative of where their locus of control lies. A person with an internal locus of control does not need the approval of others to feel good about themselves, and therefore they are more willing to accept that they are in the wrong and act.

On the other hand, a person with an external locus of control seeks validation and approval from outside, and therefore, does not like to be in a position where others may view them unfavorably which greatly affects their ability to take responsibility. Blame is the most common coping mechanism.

Why We Try to Control Factors and Place Blame

Projecting or numbing our emotions is often much easier than self-searching and finding blame in our own actions. No one likes to be wrong. We avoid feeling the uncomfortable emotions that accompany being wrong by numbing rather than evaluating what we did and acting to correct ourselves. Blaming and using excuses take the blame from us thereby making us feel good about ourselves. A 50-50 approach can help by accepting that both parties could have a share of the responsibility therefore alleviating part of the guilt without excusing the need for action

We expect life to be fair and when it isn't, we want to find who is guilty and make them pay for it. In a sense, placing blame is a way of punishing the wrong party for what they have done. This makes sense considering we often believe that actions have consequences and we feel that by taking the blame, then we must suffer the consequences of the action. This is the rationalization that often leads to mob justice; an injustice occurs, a group of people get angry and decide to find the cause of their anger so that they can make them pay for their actions.

When you consider that placing blame does not really correct the mistake made as we cannot go back in time, we find it is easier to look for a solution than to take the role of judge and jury. This does not mean that crime should go unpunished, but that the punishment should be left to the authorities not just anyone who feels wronged

When we try to take control and to place blame, we feel safe. When you know who has made a mistake and is to blame, we are able to distinguish who is 'evil' and who is 'good.' This distinction leads us to pick a side, mostly the side that is fair and true. In a way, this makes us feel that we are good people and we are safe because the guilty side is made up of bad people. This distinction is, however, wrong because nobody is perfect and making a mistake won't make you a bad person any more than being on the right side will make you a saint. We should always be objective and not try to bring in our moral judgments when mistakes occur.

Blaming creates biases which affect perceptions. As human beings, we like attributing outcomes to people and things. For many people, they attribute positive outcomes to themselves (internal attributions), and they attribute negative outcomes to external factors (external attributions). For example, passing an exam is attributed to our efforts and failure attributed to an unfair teacher or a hard exam. Another attribution error is moral luck whereby a person is only wrong if their wrong actions lead to negative outcomes.

Therefore, a person who ignores a traffic signal is considered less wrong if they do not cause an accident compared to one who causes an accident. Regardless of fault, however, perception leads us to rigid thinking as you often you find you do not want to listen to the other party. Biases create blindsides in our view and reactions and should be avoided at all costs

Blaming comes from having a perfectionist mindset. This can be greatly attributed to social media as people ruthlessly edit how they appear, so they seem perfect but rarely want to show their struggles. When we blame, we do not want to appear like we make mistakes in front of people because we assume that people will love us more if we are flawless. This is a fallacy because nobody is perfect, and we all make mistakes. We will only experience true connections with other people when we are willing to be our authentic selves and show that we are fallible, and it is okay

Blame excuses us from negative behavior and outcomes. If you fail a certain exam, the easy way out is to blame the teacher, the exam or anything else but yourself. This is because the emotions that are associated with this failure, i.e., frustration and guilt are not easy to bear. However, when you refuse to take responsibility, you also prevent yourself from learning the lesson you were supposed to learn from the situation. After all, it is not failing that is the problem but quitting. Do not let your failures deter you from trying again, be willing to learn the lesson failure is teaching you so that you do not fail in the same way again.

No matter how much we desire to control situations in our lives, we need to understand that there are some aspects of life that we will never be able to control. The following aspects can be considered:

- You cannot control natural disasters and tragedies. It is futile to fight nature and life as you will always lose.

- You cannot control the actions that happened in the past. No amount of wishing, hoping or praying will change past events.

- You cannot guarantee outcomes. You can do your best to try and get the best possible results, but beyond that, you must let them be.

- You cannot change someone's decisions and behaviors. While you can advise them, it is always up to the person to change these things.

Blame Vs. Responsibility

Placing blame is always the easiest way out of a situation. However, it doesn't solve the problem at hand. The best strategy is always to take responsibility, and this is always hard to do. We may break down the word responsibility into two words, ability and response. Responsibility is, therefore, the ability to respond to a situation so unlike blame which is always looking to the past, responsibility is always looking to the future. It is always better to take responsibility because no amount of blame can correct a situation. So rather than ask 'who did this?' or 'why did you do this?' the wiser question is 'what can we do to make this better.' Remember that personal responsibility is a choice. You cannot force it on someone else. There are many benefits to taking responsibility. They include:

- Taking responsibility always leads to fast resolution of problems compared to having to sift through witness accounts to find who is responsible for what.

- Taking responsibility takes away the feeling of helplessness and instead offers us the opportunity to correct the situation.

- Taking responsibility allows us to practice empathy and compassion rather than taking a judgmental stance.

- Taking responsibility puts you firmly in the driver's seat of your life. Rather than letting your emotions and situations control your reactions, you choose to take control of your reactions.

- Taking responsibility allows us to assess ourselves and therefore leads us to learn from our mistakes.

How Can You Take Responsibility?

- Determine the areas of your life that you can control and act on these. Learn to accept the things that you cannot control.

- Remind yourself that outcomes are a result of the event and your response. Learn to recognize and differentiate responses that lead to positive outcomes and those that lead to negative outcomes.

- Learn to differentiate between ruminating and problem-solving. Worry feeds itself, leading to more worry, but problem-solving leads you to solutions and is a more productive use of your time.

- Plan for stress management. Have strategies ready for when you feel stressed so that you know exactly what to do when you feel those uncomfortable emotions rising, for example, positive affirmations.

- Become more aware of your fears and emotions. Sometimes you realize that what you fear will happen when you take responsibility is not as bad as you think, and you can overcome it.

- Concentrate on your circle of influence. Do not get caught up needlessly worrying about things that you know you cannot influence. An example of things you can't influence is natural disasters.

The life you want will come as a result of the choices you make. Don't allow life's circumstances to dictate and control your emotions. Don't give away your power by assigning blame in situations that you can easily take responsibility and resolve. The difference between victims and victors is in how they respond to the challenges they encounter.

Stop blaming life for how your life is because it will never stop to apologize to you or to soothe you. Take the bull by the horns and refuse to be defeated. Learn to take accountability. This does not mean you beat yourself up, but that you ask what is important in that situation and you act.

When things go wrong, are you the type of person to blame God, other people, circumstances or yourself or are you the type to seek solutions? Think of a situation in the past where you rushed to point the blame. Did it make you feel better about the situation? What could you have done that would have made everything feel better?

Chapter 6:
You're Going to Die

One of the hardest things for most people to accept is that they are going to die. This is a reality that many people refuse to consider, and it is mainly because they associate death with fear and pain. Fear because they don't know when they are going to die and how or what exactly is going to happen after they die and pain because they always associate death with loss particularly that of people they love.

However, you find that those who ponder on this fact tend to do more with their lives than those who avoid it because once you accept that at some point you will not be on this planet, you begin to appreciate everyone and every moment and to live your life more deliberately.

The one harsh life lesson you must accept, and which has been accepted by every successful person, is that you will never achieve what you want most in life. Time is finite and you will die before you achieve everything you desire. Make use of the time you must do as much as you can without the temptation to put things off because you think that you will somehow have more time. If you tolerate this kind of mentality, you will never achieve anything, but if you realize that your time on earth is limited, you will act with a sense of urgency.

If you want to know what you want to do with your life, it may do you some good to consider what you would like people to remember you by, what you want to accomplish and what you want to experience before that time. While this does not diminish the fear, it makes you live your life more fully enjoying each moment and experience. You do not have the luxury of time no matter what age you are, and therefore you should strive to live each day as if it were your last— it could be.

Time is a limited precious commodity that is always moving, and you do not get a second chance. This is not a dress rehearsal, go after your dreams, tell people you love them and experience your life to the fullest. Do not let anyone tell you that it is too late to start living the life you want to live because if you are alive, you have the time. Do not put off tomorrow what you could do today.

If you wish to live your life to the fullest of your capabilities, the best place to start would be to learn time management. Time management is the deliberate planning and utilization of one's time to the best of one's ability. It is through time management that you can accomplish even your wildest dreams while still setting aside time to enjoy and have good experiences with family and friends. This life is not all about work and money, and you will find true fulfillment when you are able to make time for the things that are important to you while still going after your goals and aspirations.

Why Manage Your Time

- You need to manage our time because your time here is finite. By managing your time, you will be able to accomplish more in the time you have.

- Managing your time helps you to accomplish more things in a shorter time.

- Managing your time improves decision making as you make decisions based on how they affect your goals and your schedule.

- Managing your time increases opportunities to learn and explore as you can actively plan for them.

- Managing your time increases your chances of success as you can set routines, activities, and habits that support your goals.

- Managing your time reduces stress and overwhelm as you can plan for any tasks you have and do them before they are due.

- Managing your time teaches you discipline, particularly if you can stick to your time management plan.

- Managing your time allows you to enjoy your free time as you fit in your work during your work periods and leave out time for other things.

How to Manage Your Time

There are many time managements resources out there, but there are some universal principles of time management, and we shall discuss some of them. The best results from time management can be achieved when you take some time to track what you do so that you know how you are currently spending your time. Knowledge is power, and this knowledge will allow you to understand your natural body rhythms (when you are most active) if you have activities that occur on a daily basis and how long they take as well as understanding activities in your life that serve no purpose and need to be eliminated.

If there is something you need to do, write it down. The human brain is limited in how many things it can keep in its short-term memory bank in terms of things you say you will remember, and activities of the day could very easily overwhelm you such that you forget some of them. Some people prefer to keep a master task list that contains all the things they want to get done. Later, when you are creating daily or weekly plans, you can refer to your task list and distribute the tasks without any hustle.

There is an ongoing debate about whether a daily planner is more effective than a weekly planner. A weekly planner allows you to assign certain activities to days. For example, you could assign any creative tasks to Mondays, Wednesdays, and Fridays, allocate meetings to Tuesdays and Thursdays, assign Saturdays for fun and Sundays for planning. On the other hand, you could also assign specific hours to these tasks throughout your day, for example, mornings for creative work and afternoons for meetings and evenings for spontaneous activities. Whichever one you decide, pick one, test it out and when it doesn't work, discard and try another one.

Learn to prioritize your tasks. The best way to do this would be to use the 80/20 principle. This principle states that 80 percent of the outcomes normally come from 20 percent of effort. The percentage may fluctuate, but it is generally accepted that there are some activities that carry more weight than others. You need to find out the activities that carry the most weight and work on them first because they normally require the most effort.

Many times, you will find that by carrying out these activities first, you may eliminate the need for some of the smaller tasks or you may save them for a time when you are feeling less motivated and are more tired. Prioritization shall be expounded on more a little later in the chapter.

You need to learn to delegate. There are some things that you can do that someone else can do faster and more effectively. When you spend your time doing all the activities in your task list, you find that you get exhausted very fast and that you do not have enough, time to do the more important tasks. Some people fear delegating because they are perfectionists and often hold the view that no one can do the task as well as they can, but this is a recipe for disaster. If you want your task done in a specific way, feel free to give detailed instructions, assign the job to someone who you know can do the task well and use that time to work on other things. Delegating also works for tasks that you do not like doing, but that you can let another person do.

Avoid multitasking at all costs. You may be tempted to multitask thinking that you will accomplish the job faster. While this may be true, you often find that you do not perform the task as well as you could have had you taken the time to focus on one task at a time. When you concentrate on one task at a time, you can easily get into flow state which is where new ideas come from and which has been shown to increase the speed of learning and comprehension. Set specific times for working on a task, then commit to doing that task until it is done or until the time is up.

Avoid over-planning. Your day will rarely go exactly as you planned it. You need to schedule in time for distractions and interruptions. Your boss may give you a job to do, or a client may come in, and you find that you cannot do a certain task at the time you said you would. This is what the time you left unplanned for is for. It is also advisable that you assign only 1-3 important tasks per day. This is important because it ensures you give them your maximum effort and attention and it reduces the feeling of overwhelm you get when you have a long to-do list. You would rather go adding tasks to your to-do list from your master list as you complete them. Don't forget to plan for leisure and relaxation.

Develop A Sense of Urgency

When you have decided on how you will organize your tasks and the best time management strategy for you, it is best to create a sense of urgency in achieving your goals. The main reason is that you do not know how much time you have left, and the second reason is that it will give you motivation. A sense of urgency also helps in fostering creativity and innovation as you try to figure out which strategies will assist you to complete your goal faster. Furthermore, a sense of urgency will boost your productivity, therefore creating momentum. Developing a sense of urgency will require you to be proactive in pursuing your dreams. The following strategies can help you to create a sense of urgency.

- Break down your goals into short term and long-term milestones and set deadlines so that you can know when you are on track.

- Develop a competitive spirit. When you know that there are other entrepreneurs that are pursuing similar goals, you become more willing to put in the work to become better than them.

- You can set your own deadlines. A deadline is a good way to beat habits such as procrastination.

- Value your time. When you decide to value each moment, you will be less inclined to engage in useless activities and therefore use your time more wisely.

- Value long term rewards and pleasure over instant gratification. Binge watching your favorite show may feel good now but having a successful business will feel good for a much longer time.

- You can build an inspiring vision that is both motivating and challenging. It is important that your vision is challenging so that you feel accomplished when you achieve it.

- Build momentum. It is always harder to start than it is to maintain the momentum. When you have gained traction, you will want to keep working to make more progress.

Prioritization

When you prioritize, you distinguish between the tasks that need your attention and those that do not. The best way of prioritizing is by considering how important or urgent tasks are. Tasks that are important and urgent are crisis problems and should be handled fast and efficiently. Examples include projects with approaching deadlines. Tasks that are not urgent but are important can be delegated for example doing your laundry or mowing the lawn. A task that is neither urgent nor important, for example, watching television, can be avoided altogether or done last as they are distractions. Your focus should be on tasks that are not urgent but are important. Here you can have your daily tasks related to your goals.

Prioritization allows you to focus your time on the tasks that give you the most progress. People who prioritize their time often find that they accomplish a lot more in less time. Prioritization also means being selective about the people that you stay around. There are people that build you up and some that tear you down and when you prioritize, you will find that you will be much happier and less stressed. Make sure you prioritize work that you love. This is an easy way to beat procrastination because we often procrastinate on tasks that we do not enjoy doing. Be sure that you will have to sacrifice your time and comfort while you are pursuing your goals, but all of this will be worth it when you are successful.

We do not have as much time as we may think we do for the things we want, but this is no reason to despair. Regardless of your age or circumstances, if you begin to manage your time better, you may find you do not need to work for very long to start accomplishing your goals. It may mean that we are busy for some time, but most good things rarely come easy. Be ready to prioritize your activities and to create a sense of urgency if you want to accomplish your goals. We all have the same 24 hours in a day and those who manage theirs well always seem to achieve much more than those who do not.

Jeremy Napier

Do you have a dream you want to achieve, but that you aren't actively working towards? How can you better manage your schedule so that you are better able to do more? Sometimes it's as simple as maximizing your free time, whether it is five minutes or twenty. Little by little you will find yourself making progress towards your goals.

Chapter 7:
Never Be Satisfied

Success and wealth demand that you should be obsessed with self-improvement- never be satisfied with what you have because if you do, you will stagnate and will not have the drive to achieve more. Obsession with self-development is a healthy trait if you want to be successful and if you do not have it, it is time you developed and nurtured it in you. Success is essentially founded on the desire and willingness to grow and learn continually.

Those who are successful and wealthy perpetually believe that that change is possible even when they do not know how it will happen. Additionally, they believe that there is always something new to learn to make them better in whatever they are doing, whether knowledge or experience to give them an edge and make the more successful. It is this open and success-oriented mindset that provides fertile soil ground for self-improvement, by opening your arms to the life-altering belief in untethered possibilities and self-improvement.

To be carefree and content are bad for a wealth creation because they slow momentum and stifle the killer instinct required for success. You should always set new goals so that you have something new to aim for because human beings are goal-striving organisms and we get the most motivation and satisfaction from the process of pursuing them than we do from achieving them. It is this work ethic and undying hunger for more that will make you successful and wealthy. It should not be grandiose goals; all you need is a series of small goals to keep you focused and moving forward.

The unending hunger for more elevates your brain on a higher level of responsiveness so that you are constantly alive to opportunities that will help you achieve your goals. Self-development makes you want success so that you are compelled to do whatever is necessary to make it happen. An attitude hungry for more enables you to channel your energy and redirect it into growth energy. Think of your pursuits as a focus with purpose—those who are highly successful like you want to go there by wanting to be better and the woke up every morning thinking of how to do that and worked to get there by simply wanting more.

There is a big difference in being successful and staying hungry for success and history is replete with people who were highly successful but could not sustain the drive needed for continued success. They became very successful then disappeared because the lost the hunger- they became content with what they had. The hunger for more begins with passion, but that can only last for so long because the excitement and motivation weaken with time and must be reinvigorated. This is the reason many people find themselves losing interest or quitting, however, those who sustain success have a seemingly endless ability and determination to keep wanting more.

You need the unwavering desire to defy the challenges and keep you going even when get tough. Successful people always want more which gives them the power to overcome fears and failures the fears, the failures, the setbacks and survive the months, years or even decades of unappreciated work. Hunger for more is hard to sustain especially once you achieve success, but there are ways to feed the desire and hunger for more.

How To Stay Hungry And Self-Motivated For Success

Do Not Let Success Get in Your Head

It is very easy to forget the effort and struggle you put in to succeed once you achieve what you want. Very often, people let success get in their head because they forget the reasons, they wanted success in the first place- they show off and gloat in the success and eventually end up static. However, to remain successful and achieve more, you must remain desirous and motivated and the only way to get that is never to let success get the better of your judgment.

It is okay to be proud of your achievements and success but do not let the excitement of the moment prevent your success from working for you. Always remember that achieving success is the easy part, staying hungry after success is the hard bit.

Have the Desire to Learn More

Reading is one of the most powerful success habits and one of the top habits to boost to sustain your motivation and keep you from the illusionary satisfaction of success. The most successful people are ardent readers and so should you if you want to stay hungry. Reading won't just expand your knowledge, but it'll also keep your brain active. By reading, you are taking part in an activity that requires you to constantly process information. And this alone plays a vital role in helping you conceptualize new ideas and insights.

As you read more, you learn about various subjects from different perspectives. This understanding of perspectives goes a long way in making you flexible and open to knowledge. Keep reading and learn everything you can about your field. The more you learn, the better your mind works and the more creative and adaptable you become. The more you read, the more you know and the higher your chances of success.

This is yet another habit that won't just boost your creativity but will also help you move a step forward in achieving a growth mindset. If your mind is thoughtful and your thoughts are intelligent, you'll experience a constant urge to know and learn more. And this is exactly what you need in order to develop a growth mindset. It is your lifelong thirst for knowledge that'll truly fuel your creativity. And when you are d creative, your thoughts are bound to expand.

By taking part in a continuous process of learning, you inadvertently give your mind the much- needed ideas that help you to think better. People become broadminded by cultivating this very habit. They become broadminded as they are open to novel concepts and unique approaches. So, if you have the same goal, it's high time to start.

In order to achieve a growth mindset through creativity, you need to be willing to try unique ideas. You can't achieve this mindset if you end up dismissing everything that is beyond your comfort zone. In order to be successful, you must be open to new ideas and thoughts. So even if you disagree with something/someone, you must give them a chance to express their opinion.

Having the necessary knowledge in different areas of your life will offer you the backdrop for new ideas. At the same time, familiarity with a specific area will give you the necessary insight to work towards innovation in that specific field.

Be A Little Selfish
Staying hungry will require that you be a little selfish and think more of yourself and what is best for you. Set emotions aside and always think and settle for what is going to make you grow. This will mean that occasionally you may make decisions that will disappoint or hurt

some people, but it is all good if it will get you ahead. Successful people are always selfish people- selfish for growth not maliciously.

Gratitude: Be Thankful for Everything in Your Life

Gratitude is a key ingredient for success using the principles of the law of attraction; be grateful for what you had, for what you have, for what you are asking for and for what you are going to have. You must be forever grateful for the blessings in your life whether material or immaterial.

Jot down the things you are thankful for and always remember to thank the universe for them; just like you and I are motivated by someone's show of gratitude in appreciation for what you have done for them, so is are the laws of nature. The law of attraction is heightened more when you appreciate what it gives you.

There Is Always Room for Improvement Many people tend to think that you should put in a lot of work at the beginning and sit back to enjoy what you have achieved once you taste success, but that should not be the case. You will be more successful in practicing daily personal development.

You must that whatever you have achieved, or your abilities can be developed and improved. As much as you may not have control of external matters affecting your achievements, you most definitely have influence over the external factors that will determine whether you are successful or not. The path to success or more success is to be able to control your response to situations and to what you already have- it is a deliberate behavior and mindset change to want more.

No matter how much you have made or how much success you have achieved, there is always room to improve. By setting new goals and demanding more from of yourself, you will ignite and release the hunger to be more productive and positive that will give you the ability to get anything you want. The limit is up to you-you are the decider of how much you achieve.

The other reason why you must strive for more is the inescapable fact that the world around you is changing; what was latest in terms of information, technology, demand, etc. yesterday is not necessarily what is relevant today.

To be flexible enough to be able to change with the times and demands of the fluid world around you, because the world is in constant change, you must be willing to learn and must have an internal desire for more. Keep looking for opportunities instead of worrying about the risks or being content with what you have so far. If you can shift your mindset to never be satisfied, you should be able to realize more success.

Chapter 8:
Go Big or Go Home

Take a chance! All life is a chance. The man who goes the furthest is generally the one who is willing to do and dare." – Dale Carnegie

Many people do not sustain success because they are turned off by risks, but the hard things are just that, risks, and require that you should not be afraid to make hard decisions. You must go big or go home for money wealth success mindset because it is what distinguishes long term success from one-off success. Risk takers are much more likely to be successful than those who are afraid to take the jump because they are not limited and are willing to channel their energy to make things happen.

To achieve great things, you must be willing to go outside of your comfort zone to reap the rewards that come from taking risks. Unfortunately, many of us find it difficult to deal with the uncertainty that accompanies risk-taking because they are overwhelmed with the fear and unease of potential failure. The point of risk-taking is not in the outcome but the experiences and lessons from the process. As much as taking risks could lead to failure, it will help you confront your fears.

We always underestimate our ability to handle the consequences of taking risks; therefore, we often let our doubts get the better of us. As a result, we shy away from taking on new challenges or pursuing new opportunities because we don't trust ourselves sufficiently. The consequence is that we end up underutilizing our capacity for risks and thus block off our success.

Sticking with the status quo does not help because the cost of inaction is way greater and leads to deep regret than any failure you may be faced with as you pursue success. Do not delude yourself with the false hope that circumstances will get better without acting nor should you come up with excuses for not making the necessary moves. Playing safe is bad for wealth creation and success because the things that are not working out now will mostly get worse with time. So, learn to overcome the urge to play safe and keep forging ahead.

Successful People Differentiate Themselves by Doing What's Difficult and Taking Risks for Big Rewards

The first step to winning big is to accept the potential for failure and embrace it. Fear has no place in the journey for wealth and success. You may view failure negatively, but it is a great tool for building a success-oriented mindset by exposing us to experiences where we can learn and by making us resilient and strong. If you are truly passionate about your goals and vision, the more the persistence and perseverance to achieve them will grow. Taking risks does not guarantee success every time; however, it guarantees that you will be a better person because of it and will boost your resilience to recover quickly from difficult situations.

Successful people are overconfident because of the lessons learned and the character built from the difficulties they have faced along the way. Take big chances without fearing the outcome- either way, you will learn through the process and build the skills which will improve your chances of achieving future goals. If you ever want to achieve your dreams start taking calculated risks. Risk taking will enrich your life and make your pursuits more rewarding. The benefits of taking risks:

- You are much more likely to have better defined and set goals when you take calculated risks. Risk taking leads to careful thought and compels you to make things work to achieve what you want.

- Risk taking leads to more success than not taking the plunge. By giving your best and put everything you can into reaching a goal, you have a higher likelihood of getting it done.

- Once you are a risk-taker, your mindset will shift from the safe approach to a more success-oriented hungry mindset which will help you to achieve more success. You will boost your self-confidence which will enable you to take on new challenges without doubt or fear. If you are willing to take risks, you will be exposed to new challenges and opportunities which will force you to learn new skills.

- Risk-takers are empowered to establish new mental limits beyond their comfort zone; you will be able to achieve more when you expand your boundaries and comfort zone.

- You become more creative because you commit to solving a problem wholeheartedly despite the challenges thus opening your mind to new ideas.

You Can't Stay in Your Comfort Zone Forever If You Want Success

Goal setting achievement and success requires sacrifices and a shift of some things in your life- if you are not willing to make changes in your life, you cannot be successful at achieving your goals. Clawing on to our comfort zones is probably the biggest hindrance to us achieving what we set out to do. Nobody likes to change and certainly the kind of change that success demands, it will always feel easier to maintain the status quo rather than make the shift to get you to where you dream of being.

Once the comfort zone overpowers us, the inclination is to postpone or forget what we intended to pursue. Before you know it, it is

November, and you have not achieved any of the things you resolved to do at the beginning of the year. Complacency is the main reason for our inclination to remain where we are comfortable, and it is important to break free of them for money wealth and success mindset. You should make whatever adjustments required to help you succeed, focus on the target and not the hardships to get you there.

One of the main reasons why people are afraid to accept new challenges is because they fear the possibilities of failure. All of us aren't strong. So instead of finding opportunity in a challenge, we usually focus on the impact of failure. This mentality is the sole reason why we stumble and stutter before taking on something new. The possibilities of failure weigh us down, so we try avoiding a challenge and instead follow the same path as before. We make inane excuses in order to avoid a challenge. We do everything possible to avoid getting out of our comfort zones.

But staying in a comfort zone solely because of fear isn't as comfortable as you'd assume. By avoiding a specific challenge, you're missing out on the opportunity to learn about yourself and understand your abilities better. You'll feel perennially trapped. It's almost like you're living a life that isn't true to your own potential. Your mind is clouded by thoughts discomfort, unhappiness, anxiety, and a crippling sense that things should be different.

And this is exactly why you need to accept the challenge and try to make the most out of it. In order to lead a life of mindfulness, with a growth mindset, you'll have to accept the new challenges that come your way. After all, it is these challenges that'll give you better opportunities in helping you assume your true self. Yes, you will be afraid. You will fear to step out of your comfort zone. But if you're really looking to grow as an individual, you'll have to rise above this fear, take the challenge, and use it to its maximum potential.

Things You Can Do to Help You Get out of Your Comfort Zone

Identify Your Passion and Purpose

Before you embark on setting any goals, you need to find a purpose for your life on which to align and use as the basis of your goals and pursuits. For you to be fulfilled and enjoy what you are doing or relish pursuing your goals, it is critical that you first find your true passion and purpose. When you do not have a purpose for your life on which to base your desires and goals, you basically lack the compass to guide you through life, and you may end up not being motivated enough to pursue the goals you have set for yourself.

Your purpose determines why you want to pursue the goals you set for yourself so that you are fulfilled in the end.

Finding and acknowledging life's purpose is the most important thing you can do and is the main difference between success and failure. When we fall short of our goals, in most cases, we do not have a clear purpose for which we are doing the things we do to inculcate a sense of urgency or ownership of what we are doing. Without a purpose, it does not really matter whether you succeed or not.

A clear purpose will help you to understand what you want and then drive you to pursue it enthusiastically and passionately. Finding a purpose for some people is very easy because they are born with clear talents which can be developed, nurtured and pursued while for others, it is not so easy to pinpoint where their passion lies and will need some soul searching to settle on a purpose.

Your purpose should be something you are passionate about. The first step in finding your purpose is to do a self-assessment to find out what you want to do with your life.

Positive Affirmations

Dr. Wayne Dyer says- "You do not attract what you want, you attract what you are." Take a minute to think about it. If you are unhappy, even if you strive to attract happiness it will not happen, you must be happy in thought and mind for you to attract more happiness into your life. Whatever you affirm consciously with complete feelings will give you the emotional experience in your mind. Choose to affirm the good things in your life instead of dwelling on the bad and bask in the joy of living the harmonious and happy life that you are seeking.

You must have a burning desire for what you want, which is only triggered by your thoughts and mind; otherwise, the law will not work for you. Let your passion for the life or things you want to be unstoppable; think about it every day until it turns into a burning desire! For you to continually and positively think about your desires, employ the use of autosuggestions and affirmation techniques. Autosuggestions are the means by which we sway our subconscious mind to enable the manifestation of our desires; jot down your powerful affirmations and go through them regularly. A positive affirmation will be something like:

"I believe that I will get everything I want, and I know that I will get all I ask for. I know it!"

Affirmations and autosuggestions act by convincing your subconscious mind that they are the ultimate truth which strengthens your faith further. These are probably the biggest weapons you can have when it comes to cultivating constant positive thoughts. You must know that your mind is a bank for thoughts; if you have positive thoughts, good feelings grow while with negative thoughts, the contrary is true. Negative thoughts will drain your mental bank of the positivity that was deposited there leaving you burdened by negative energy and despair.

Set and Review Goals Regularly to Motivate You

The goals you set for yourself must be those that will motivate you. They must be important to you and your vision, and there must be a value to you in achieving them. The goals you set should be connected to the things which hold a high priority in your life so that you are assured that you will stay focused to achieve them. Without the type of focus triggered by high priority, you may end up with many goals thus lacking enough time to devote to each.

If your interest in the outcome of a goal is limited or the goal is not relevant or necessary in the larger context, the likelihood of being committed to it and staying focused to see it through is greatly diminished. Achieving goals requires a commitment to achieve—to maximize the chances of success, a sense of urgency must be elicited in you. Without a must-do attitude, you risk not doing all that is needed to accomplish the goal.

As you ponder and come up with your goals, ensure that every goal is motivating and write down on paper why the goal is important to you. Goal setting is basically the process of realizing accomplishment, if done correctly, the impact on your success will be very powerful.

Interact with successful people you want to emulate and can be accountable to.

As much as the goals you are pursuing are yours, it is recommended that you share your endeavor and be accountable to someone to ensure that you keep the flames of commitment and persistence alive. This entails sharing your goals and declaring your commitment to someone who is close to you and who supports your intentions like a partner, mentor, parent, etc. It is much easier to keep pursuing our goals when we know that there is someone assessing us or one who will expect a progress report.

When searching for an accountability partner, you should keep in mind that the right person is someone who will challenge, engage and inspire a sense of accomplishment in you to be able to succeed. The ideal person should be one who you admire for his or her accomplishments. Look for your partner through a deliberate effort so that you find the right match for your needs and goals.

The concept of the accountability partner has been with us for ages, and it is not surprising that the most successful people at achieving their goals engage an accountability partner. This person will be your trusted confidant or mentor whom you can trust and will guide you and motivate you to keep on the right track.

Everyone Can Do the Easy Things; Not Many People Can Do the Hard Tasks for Success

Industriousness is an essential ingredient for success and wealth creation and like somebody said, success is the travel partner of hard work, and there are not two ways about it. You must be willing to work hard and to go the extra mile even after success to achieve more to be truly successful and to create the wealth that we all desire.

However, it is not just hard work for the sake of it. It should be that you work hard within a clearly defined action plan with detailed milestones to help you get what you want but to allow for progress monitoring as well. The only way of knowing whether you are succeeding or not is to be able to reliably monitor your effort.

Be passionate about your pursuits and like everything that you do- you have a higher chance of success if you are happy about what you are doing. Everyone can do the easy things, and that is why most of us are yet to reach our full potential and achieve success. The successful people are the ones who do what everyone else does not want to do because it is hard. So, be a hard worker, and you will see your success and wealth creation dreams turn into reality sooner than you know it.

Chapter 9:
Positive Optimism

Optimists are the people who chose to expect the best in life while pessimists expect that things will always go wrong. In other terms, optimists concentrate on the donut while pessimists obsess on the hole. It all comes down to their mindset. Humans are wired to expect and avoid negative outcomes. This is because when we were hunters and gatherers, those who erred on the side of caution were less likely to become prey to wild animals. However, in the modern setting, looking for the negative side of things serves to increase your misery and prevent you from taking new risks.

In this chapter, we shall look at what positive optimism can teach you about the power of a self-made millionaire mindset. You will know why if you project positive thoughts, then anything is possible, so it will really drive you to achieve more. The reason for millionaire success is in their mindset - as millionaires achieve more and more, their thoughts are deliberately more positive and bigger. They think about the potential future which drives their creativity and desire to be creative and successful.

If you desire to pursue a goal, it is much better to think big. Thinking small prevents you from assessing the possibilities, and we are at an age where entrepreneurs try to outwit each other by providing the best services. There are many reasons why things could go wrong, but there is always the possibility that things could work out in your favor and it is up to you to decide which view you prefer. Do not get bogged down by pros and cons lists, looking at the statistics of how many people have failed before you or trying to create realistic expectations, open your mind up to creativity and innovative ideas. Just make sure that you are ready to put in the work to make your ideas a reality.

In many studies about self-made millionaires, it is a common trend to find that many of them knew that they would succeed. They tend to be optimistic and enthusiastic individuals. Some of the richest people of our time became rich by executing ideas that seemed absurd when they were starting out but that later bring them great success. They have very open-minded views to ideas always trying to see how an idea can be implemented in order to work and always brainstorming on problem-solving.

In fact, it is not uncommon to find that when they were starting out, they had more people tell them that their dreams were not realistic, but they were daring enough to start anyway and resilient enough to stick it out through the challenges in order to get to where they are today.

Benefits of Optimism

Optimists are less lonely than pessimists because of their enthusiastic nature. Optimists generally respond enthusiastically to people and situations, and they always look for ways to turn obstacles into steppingstone. This quality is very attractive to people and, therefore optimists always find that they attract many people to them. On the other hand, pessimists always seem to be pushing people away from them leading to social exclusion. This may be explained by the fact that many people view pessimists as having toxic attitudes and prefer to stay away from them. Pessimists can find problems in almost any situation and are often complaining and whining leading to negative attitudes that always bring people down

Optimists enjoy more achievements and success in their lives. This may be explained by the fact that they have positive expectations about the future and because the subconscious mind brings forth our most dominant thoughts, they manifest their success. It may also be because they are expecting success so they become more motivated to work on their goals so that they can make their expectations a reality. A pessimist will find possible problems in any goal and therefore not feel as motivated to work hard as they are expecting to fail anyway. Optimists have also been found to get more job offers and promotions, and the reason may be because they are more likable than pessimists and because they expect to get these jobs and promotions

Jeremy Napier

Optimists are more resilient when they face problems. This is a very important quality in life and in business because problems are a part of life. The outcome of any situation is always determined by the response of an individual to the negative event. A pessimist will resign themselves to the problem, ruminating and whiling and otherwise justifying their expectations about things going wrong. An optimist, on the other, hand looks for the lesson to be learned in the situation, then begins to find ways to solve the problem or use it to their advantage. They justify the saying that it's not how many times you get knocked down, but how many times you pick yourself up, dust yourself off and try again

Optimism fosters self-confidence. When a person is optimistic, they have hope that their future is going to be bright. If you have a business idea that you want to execute and that you feel optimistic about, you will have confidence in yourself. When you overcome challenges and don't let them bog you down, your self-confidence will increase. On the other hand, pessimists don't always feel confident in themselves or their dreams because they are always expecting things to go wrong and waiting for the other proverbial shoe to drop. It is difficult to feel confident about your future when you expect to fail and as a result pessimist's thoughts are full of fear and trepidation.

Optimism fosters creativity and innovation. People who are optimistic tend to have big dreams that they are hopeful will come true. This leads them to imagine new and inventive ways of making their dreams come true. This innovation is also useful in solving problems because they generally refuse to be defeated by their problems. Pessimists, on the other hand, tend to have a very narrow-minded view of life. They spend a lot of time dreading the outcomes and even more time ruminating on problems when they arise that they rarely allow themselves to see how they could turn those problems into ideas.

Optimists are better at stress management and tend to be healthier. This is because they view problems as opportunities and do not let situations bother them as much as they bother pessimists. In health, it has been found that they enjoy more health because they generally do not expect to get sick, they expect to recover faster when they are sick and seem to have higher pain thresholds than pessimists. It is because of this that medical practitioner's general refrain from performing surgeries on people that are depressed as depressed people have negative expectations. Furthermore, optimists tend to have lower blood pressure. This is because stress increases blood pressure and optimists generally manage their stress better by reacting better to stressful situations.

Optimists take more calculated risks than pessimists. Whenever optimists have an idea, they look for ways to manifest these ideas to reality. This means that they are often more open to new sometimes risky strategies and ideas that they feel increase their chances of success. Pessimists on the other hand already anticipate defeat and often tend to play it safe. Generally, pessimists have been noted to engage in bad risks such as experimenting with drugs and bad behaviors for the immediate thrill that they provide. This may be because pessimism never leads to the production of the feel-good hormones (endorphins, serotonin, and dopamine) released when someone thinks happy thoughts or contemplates a positive outcome, but these risks do.

Optimists tend to take more responsibility for their lives. They take greater measures to improve their circumstances, they are much happier and are better at stress management. This is because they are normally looking forward to the future and rarely ruminate on their past unless they are contemplating what lessons they learned. Pessimists tend to judge their lives based on how their past was and how things 'never seem to work out.' This way of living their lives often makes them feel powerless to change their circumstances leading to negative dispositions. In this sense, pessimists tend to act like the victims in their lives while optimists tend to take charge of their lives.

How to Be More Optimistic
Perhaps the best place to start is to decide to be optimistic. Optimism is an attitude and, as such, it is a choice. Just as one can choose to see how a situation can go wrong, you can choose to concentrate on how the same situation can succeed. You can decide to face each obstacle as a stumbling block, or you can decide to look at each situation as a steppingstone. In the words of Winston Churchill, "The pessimist

sees difficulty in every opportunity. The optimist sees opportunity in every difficulty'" Optimism is a choice, and it is entirely up to you

You can learn to be more optimistic by associating with more people who you recognize as optimists and disassociating with pessimists. You are the sum of the people you stay around, and if you become deliberate about the kind of people you let into your circle, you will find that their enthusiasm seeps into your life. Sometimes the people that are pessimistic are your family or your coworkers, and you may not be able to stay away from them completely. In that case, it is advisable that you begin limiting the times you spend with them, and you keep from expressing your ideas to them so that they do not affect your optimism towards these ideas.

You can learn stress management techniques that remind you to keep negative thinking (pessimism) away. Meditation, yoga and deep breathing techniques are some excellent ways to teach your brain to keep calm. They reduce stress in your body by lowering your blood pressure and calming your brain. When you are calmer, you're better able to think of solutions and contemplate deliberate reactions to situations. Another very effective method is using positive affirmations to remind you to keep calm. Examples include 'I can do it,' 'This too shall pass,' and 'I am always calm.' The affirmations can be repeated in front of the mirror, out loud or even silently until you feel calmer

Another easy way to be optimistic is to be conscious of the information you feed yourself. If you want to be more optimistic, you are better off reading motivational books, articles, and messages. You can watch positive videos online or on YouTube, and you can listen to tapes and podcasts by people who have positive attitudes or by listening to upbeat music. It is also advisable that you filter out negative information by not watching the news or reading the newspapers too often. This is because a lot of news today is negatively geared towards raising viewership. If you work in a field that requires you to be updated on the news, you can refrain from reading the news early in the morning or late in the evening as they affect how you start your day and how you sleep respectively.

Exercise is another simple way to be more optimistic. Exercising makes your brain produce feel-good hormones that make you feel happier and more enthusiastic. Regular exercise will keep you feeling happy which is on top of the fact that you will be healthier. When we exercise, we tend to feel good about ourselves and our bodies and this enthusiasm can lead us to work harder so that we can create a better future for ourselves. Couple this with making healthy food choices, sleeping better and drinking more water and you will find yourself more energized and motivated to pursue your dreams.

You should be careful to temper your optimism with action. Positive thinking that is not followed by actual action is actually wishful thinking, and it will get you nowhere. You should also pair your optimism with integrity in that you look for the best outcomes in any situation, but you consider the current facts and situations. You are more trustworthy and respected when you can present the current facts as they are even as you strive towards making a situation better? This is particularly important in business so that you do not seem overconfident and make promises you cannot deliver.

Optimism is a mindset characterized by the ability to envision a future full of possibilities and to work towards that future. If you have goals that you want to pursue, it is important that you believe that you can achieve them. This is because we live in a limitless universe in which almost anything is possible and because it does you no good to be pessimistic. Optimism is a characteristic possessed by most of the richest people in the world. It is a very attractive quality that attracts customers and investors alike and keeps you from despairing when problems arise. Remember that it is easy to be pessimistic, but it is optimism that gets you out of the problem.

When things go wrong as they often do, do you find yourself ruminating on the fact that things went wrong, or do you find yourself asking what you can do to make the situation better. The first reaction is the ultimate sign of pessimism while the second is a sign of optimism. Does the pessimistic thought help the situation in any way?

Chapter 10:
Haters Criticism

If you want to be successful, you must be ready to deal with your hater's criticism because you are bound to face them. You must develop the attitude, mentality, and stomach to handle both positive and negative criticism but especially the negative comments. Success attracts attention and with-it people who will hate you for a variety of reasons, most of which you will not know or even understand. No successful person escapes criticism and neither will you.

Success draws in both admirers and critics. Your haters will be ranting against you because of jealousy or envy, therefore, do not be shocked about it. Be prepared enough to take the criticism and strong enough to work through them and get even more success- the best way of treating criticism is to use it as a motivator to enable you to achieve more. Everywhere you look, especially on social media, successful people are bombarded with harsh and unwarranted criticism.

Now that you are on your way to even more success, it is best that you learn about criticism and prepare to deal with it. As much as it is harsh, criticism is an equally positive tool which you can exploit to boost your personal growth and overall success. Many motivational coaches and speakers will tell you that if you want to achieve great success, you must be willing to be hated. First, you need to understand the people you will be dealing with, the haters.

These are basically people who are angry or venting out their pent-up frustrations, which is a sign of their emotional vulnerability and weakness. Simply put, these are people who do not like you because you have achieved what they want and cannot get.

The question you ought to be asking yourself to evaluate your ability to withstand the potential hate is whether you are willing to be criticized to get what you want. If you want to escape hater's criticism, the sure way of doing it is by doing nothing, and you know too well where that will lead you. The only one who cannot be criticized is one who does nothing. Hater's criticism is the price you pay for success so, do not let the noise of the naysayers get to you, you must be onto something good that is why you are attracting their attention.

Remember, not everyone will share in your happiness, and you should accept this for a money wealth success mindset. The most important thing in dealing with criticism is how you will deal with it- you should use the negative energy as a motivator to drive you to do more or better. Never let criticism and hate deflate your self-confidence and derail you from your goals. Indeed, if you approach hater's criticism as any other feedback you have received before, you will overcome it.

Think about it- what do you use the other feedback you get? Well, you use it to evaluate where you are to help you adjust get you to where you want to get. Approach negative criticism the same way. In fact, it is possible to find some genuinely helpful feedback in hater's comments.

To Be Successful Means Being Different

You are inviting hater's criticism because you are different—you are successful, and you are thinking out of the box. It is this difference, which is attracting the criticism and, ironically, the same thing that has made you as successful as you are. So, embrace the fact that you are unique and are certainly different from those who are not as successful as you. Here are some things that make successful people different from everybody else:

- They concentrate and focus on the purpose for which they are pursuing a goal rather than dwelling on the challenges along the way.

- Your haters are hoping to see you fail and you will have a few setbacks on your way to success and even after succeeding. Success is for those who can pull themselves back up from failure, learn from them and turn the experiences into catalysts for more success.

- Successful people have no place in their lives for satisfaction as you have already learned in chapter 7. Keep asking yourself "What next?" if you want to sustain success. Never allow yourself to be comfortable with what you have.

- Challenges, frustrations, and obstacles are simply viewed as small inconveniences along the way to the big price. Do not allow them to deflate your drive, rather, use them to fuel it.

- Successful people value their dreams deeply that they are not bothered by hater's criticism or do not care to please others.

As much as you may find it difficult to stomach negative criticism, you can use it to strengthen your character and for self-improvement. Like has been said earlier, criticism is a price of your success but do not be afraid of it because it will only make you stronger. Here is how hater's criticism can be beneficial:

Use the Hate to Emotionally Charge
Rather than allowing harsh criticism to make you feel small and worthless turn passion around and use it to positively charge emotionally. Do what you must do to succeed, rise above the hate and use the energy to drive you forward.

Motivate You to Define Your Goal Clearly
Use the hate to help you be clear and better focused on what you want to achieve. Once you define what you want and why you want it, no

amount of criticism can sway you. Use their energy to propel you and forward to achieve your dreams. Show them more success by feeding off their energy.

Keeps You Humble

When you are bombarded with hate and negativity, you will cherish success but will be humbled at the same time by the attention you garner and how many people are watching your success journey. Use this as a motivator and to inspire you to show the haters what they can achieve if they only channeled the energy, they are expending on must better themselves.

Helps You Understand That You Are Getting It Right

Rather than get annoyed and get into verbal sparring with your haters, this can be a lesson in taking the high road and doing what is right. Having haters means you are doing something right and succeeding because you cannot have haters if you are not doing well. What would they be hating you for?

A Lesson in Being More Accepting and Tolerant

Once you have experienced it, you will know how it feels and should not do it to another. More importantly, you can point it out if someone is being hateful and will make you empathetic to others. More importantly, by going through it and overcoming it, you are in the best position to advise and motivate people who are facing a similar situation and are having a difficult time.

Use the Criticism for Self-Evaluation

Sometimes, the criticism is well-founded and even if it is not, spend a bit of time to evaluate yourself against the accusations. Listen to what they are saying, discard the useless comments and embrace the constructive ones. Criticism can make you a better person.

Use Them to Learn How to Deal with Conflict

Hate and negative comments are a good opportunity to learn how to handle conflict—dealing with the challenges of haters teaches you how to handle difficult situations and to navigate conflict.

Anger Management

There is no better platform for learning how to cope with anger that when faced with criticism from your haters. This is the best place to learn to respond calmly or not respond at all when faced with negative comments and to temper your anger.

Ignoring Negativity

One of the habits required for success is a positive mindset. If you are not strong enough to deal with the negativity from your haters, you are basically falling off the positive mindset. Your haters can help you deal with and ignore negative situations to maintain a positive mentality to help you succeed.

Motivation for Success

As already indicated above, you should use the haters to motivate you to fly even higher. There is no better motivation than to use the negativity of the naysayers to drive your determination and persistence to achieve what you want.

To conclude, all you need to do is to keep in mind that hater's criticism is just that- do not give it a lot of premium because it should not keep you from pursuing your goals. Giving in to the whims of your haters or playing into their hands is very easy if you do not keep your guard up and stay focused. You will encounter many hurdles on the journey to success including hate, take it as recognition of your work and a cue to keep working hard. Let hate be the fuel that propels you to greater heights rather than bringing you down.

Chapter 11:
Never Tap Out

The first rule of success is to never tap out no matter what. Quite often, when we are faced with hard times on the journey to success, we are tempted to give up because it is always the easiest option. The pursuit of success is not an easy journey and you must be prepared to fail before you can succeed when things get tough, that is the time to work twice as hard instead of giving up.

We all get the feeling of despair and doubt when things get tough. Whatever goals you want to achieve, big or small, you will face challenging periods where your commitment and motivation will be tested to seemingly impossible limits. This is when self-doubt creeps in, and you start feeling hopeless, but it is important to remember that the tough times are periodical, they never last. When you have a purpose behind your goals and targets, quitting should not be an option. When you believe in your pursuit strongly, you will have the perseverance to overcome the challenges which may prompt you to quit.

The thing with giving in to the temptation to quit is that you will be left wondering for the rest of your life what would have been if you hang in there. If you want to succeed, you must have the heart to persevere and face the most difficult temptations on your journey to success. One thing is for sure; if you quit, you can be sure of not achieving your goals.

Why You Should Never Give Up on Yourself

There is no room for giving up for money wealth success mindset. Giving up is by miles the MAIN reason why most people will not be successful and is the main difference between success and failure!

Interestingly, the opposite is the irrefutable reason why only 1% become extraordinary or successful - they do not tap out! While most of us are left wallowing in regret and lost opportunities, why we never pursued a dream or goal, the 1% who had the courage and mental temerity to deal with challenges and obstacles and keep going enjoy the fruits of money, wealth, and success.

You Are Bigger Than the Temptation to Quit

Your purpose and goals are greater than the temptation to quit. The effort and hard work that you have put into your journey for success are greater than the challenges you are facing. Challenges are temporary, believe in yourself and remember that the tough times do not last forever.

It Is All Mental

The decision to quit or to stay fighting is all about your mindset- failure or success depends on how strong you are mentally to face problems and overcome them.

Success Is Not an Easy Journey
Just to remind you- success is not a bed of roses. It requires hard work and a lot of patience to see through. Be prepared to cope with whatever life throws at you.

Success Is Not Instantaneous
Success is a long patient process. Overnight success is a myth- if you come into the journey for success with the mentality of striking it rich overnight, you are a lot likely to fall off by the wayside. Many people assume that successful people got to where they are overnight, however, if you asked them you will find that their journey to success is replete with failures and setbacks that were only surmounted because of their undeterred desire for success.

You Will Make Quitting A Habit
Give up once, and you will leave behind a trail of half-done, half achieved aspirations and goals. It is very easy to make failure a habit, and like all habits is perfected by repetition.

How to Not Give Up and Stay Motivated
Focus and motivation are important for the pursuit and achievement of goals. In order to stay motivated in the journey to success, you need unwavering dedication to enable you to accomplish the goals

you have set. Because there is no quick solution to achieving goals to fulfill our purpose and vision, it requires continuous work to transform your goal into an accomplishment, which calls for sustained focus. Focus helps you to manifest your goals so that it becomes easier to reach them. Here are some things you can do to sustain your focus and motivation to achieve your goals:

Keep Negative Thoughts at Bay

Negative thoughts are bad for the achievement of goals. Negative thoughts should be kept at bay and must be replaced with thoughts of success and positive affirmations. You cannot possibly succeed at anything if all you think about is negative. Look for positive things and the little successes even during failure.

Know That It Is Okay to Fail

Nobody expects you to be successful all the time and nor should you. Accept and know that it is okay to fail and that you will probably fail a few times in the pursuit of your goals. Your aim should be to do your best in order to achieve your goals. If for whatever reason you do not achieve your set goals consider it a temporary setback and focus on the gains made, however few, and use the lessons learned for future success.

Accept That You Are the One Responsible for Your Success

No excuses or finger pointing success or failure in the pursuit of your goals is your sole responsibility. Once you realize that you have the power to make or break your achievements, you will always be alive to the importance of the process and will ensure that your goals are achieved.

Do Not Be Too Hard on Yourself

There is no place for perfection in the pursuit of money and if you want to succeed. Be your own number one supporter and always encourage yourself to move forward. Beating yourself too hard when you fall short will only undermine your focus and motivation.

Forget the Past

So, you failed to get one of your milestones right or did not meet a deadline- do not let this hang over your shoulder forever and prevent you from going forward in confidence. Challenges are part of the process, get up and keep moving. Bad feelings and memories encourage negative thoughts- it is important to work through shortcomings and do not let the past determine your future.

Focus on The Possible

DO not be unrealistic or overambitious- to sustain your focus, concentrate on the possible. Work on the things that you can do while always evaluating and reminding yourself of your abilities and positive qualities.

Being Consistent

To be consistent means that you must be willing to go all the way to commit and dedicate yourself to acting over the long-term to achieve your goals. It means that you can withstand and overcome distractions to keep your eyes on the price and it comes down to being repetitive; consistency requires that you repeat the same habits over and over until they become second nature because it trains the brain to engage in the ritual that will help you to achieve your goals. It makes it easier for your brain to convert a repeated behavior into a habit if you engage in it every day.

Learn from Your Failures and Get Back Up

Instead of looking at failure as something that is so bad and the end of our pursuits, you need to flip it on its head and treat it as an experience and opportunity for you to learn. Look closely for the lessons that you can learn from your setbacks and use them to boost your pursuit of for success and wealth. Learning from your failures will empower you with the skills to be resilient and face future setbacks. You only fail if you quit, therefore; it goes without saying that if you do not quit failure cannot be a part of your vocabulary. Do not let the fear of failure stop you from pursuing your purpose.

Achieving success is never a smooth journey; you will be met with challenges and obstacles on the way to achieving your goal, and it requires that you are mentally prepared for these eventualities so that you are not driven off course or you are not overwhelmed to the point of quitting. Whatever your goal is, small or a big, you must be prepared that there are times ahead times when you will deal with tough hurdles and even failure but do not give up.

The difference between failure and success for those who are on the journey to success is the mental strength to face and overcome challenges that may arise.

You start by accepting and acknowledging that there will be hurdles along the way to your goal. Therefore, prepare yourself mentally to meet and overcome any obstacles before you start on the journey to success. You should find the means to deal with and overcome any roadblocks. Even though it can be really frustrating at times as you work towards your goals, you need to learn how to encourage yourself despite your trials. Here are ways to help you face goal-setting roadblocks successfully:

Identify Possible Obstacles
One of the things you should do as you embark on the journey to wealth creation is to evaluate your goals for the potential roadblock you may encounter. It is impossible to foresee everything, but there are many hindrances that you can anticipate if you take the time to carefully interrogate the goals you have picked.

As much as we do not want to think about the potential roadblocks, part of effective goal setting planning is to identify potential obstacles and outline ways of dealing and overcoming them. Anticipating problems and identifying them will help you to come up with an action plan that includes putting out the potential fires. Make a list in advance of any potential hurdles you may encounter them create a contingency plan to deal with them. Obstacles are both internal and external, for example, a lack of money is external while fear and self-doubt are internal obstacles.

Recognize The 'False Hope Syndrome'

False hope syndrome is what has been described as setting a goal, being surprised by the effort it requires and giving up on it. People experience false hope when they expect quick results but realize that it will not be the case. Do not get carried away when setting goals, instead, you have to remember to be realistic and that there are goals which take time and will require that you set clear mini-goals and timelines to help you avoid unrealistic expectations and stay focused. Setting small goals and celebrating the small successes can help stay focused by keeping your momentum going.

Treat Challenges as Learning Experiences

It has been shown that people who treat challenges as an opportunity to learn are more likely to have a positive view of their ability to accomplish their goals. To stay focused on the positive side of goal setting, do not beat yourself up over failures but quickly learn from the experience and looking forward to the future. It is not that people who are successful do not face setbacks or have fewer obstacles as compared to those who give up, the only difference is how those who walk out of obstacles positively view the situation.

Do Not Be A Perfectionist

The preoccupation with perfectionism can also distract you and interfere with your focus. Do not hold yourself to unrealistic standards because you will be left feeling like your goals cannot be achieved. Do not push yourself too hard- be compassionate with yourself and always remind yourself that like everyone else you can be faced with challenges and can make mistakes.

Positive thinking is effective at helping people adapt and learn, rather than focus on the negative aspects of mistakes, rather, remind yourself that no matter how unpleasant, every setback is a learning experience.

Stay Passionate
Stay passionate- as simple as that. To maintain the necessary focus on your goals, ensure that you keep the drive and passion burning. Remembering what you are aiming for will help you stay focused for goal setting success despite any prevailing difficulties.

Revise Your Goals
Sometimes all that is requires to stay driven and on track is a revision of your goals. Your goals may need reconfiguration to keep you interested and to set them afresh, include new plans or even do away with some completely.

The question of sustained focus is a question of attitude. With the right attitude, you will have the mental focus to remain alert to the goal setting process and to improve your chances of achieving success.

The question of how to stay focused and motivated to achieve your goals is simply how you can influence and nurture the right attitude within yourself.

The focus is important for the pursuit and achievement of goals. In order to stay focused throughout the goal setting process, you need unwavering dedication and motivation to enable you to accomplish the goal you have set. Because there is no quick solution to achieving goals to fulfill our purpose and vision, it requires continuous work to transform your goal into an accomplishment, which calls for sustained focus. Focus helps you to manifest your goals so that it becomes easier to reach them.

Focus and motivation are not easy to sustain, yet they are the elements which ensure that you stay the course to achieve your goals successfully. Adapting these tips and many others will help to remind you of the importance of your goals and will help to keep you focused and motivated to succeed so that your vision is realized.

Setbacks are inescapable and must be expected in any endeavor. Roadblocks should not be the end of your goal setting journey and should not be a reason to automatically deter you from your goals. Analyze and find out why you are facing a setback if it is something you can control go ahead and deal with it, if you cannot, find a way around it that will not force you to abandon your dream.

Stay focused by finding new opportunities from the hurdles you face. As you have undoubtedly heard, some of the most successful things were never planned. Persevere by reminding yourself of past successes to lift your spirit and determination. Setbacks should fuel you to strive harder to be successful at your goals. Never tap out.

Chapter 12:
Millionaire Success Hacks

"Opportunity greets everyone at least once or twice in everyone's life, but if opportunity doesn't find you ready to expand and grow, it will come in your front door and leave out the window." – Matt Rushbrook

These are the top hacks used by the most successful people to get them to the top and keep them there. Success requires preparation as much as it demands that you work hard to achieve it. Your thoughts determine how successful you are thus the importance of millionaire success hacks which will basically work on your mindset. Controlling your emotions and thoughts is the beginning of your success.

Time Is Money

Have the most respect for time because like the old proverb goes time is more valuable than the money you want and to create wealth you need to make the best use of the limited time you have. Learn how valuable time is for success and you will be surprised at how much and profoundly you will realize positive change.

Being time conscious is the one money, wealth, and success mindset hack that will instantly create inner drive like no others and make you the hardest worker in the room. Once you are conscious to the ephemeral nature of time and its scarcity, you will commit to get things done now, rather than later.

Successful people have discovered and embraced the importance of time. It is for this reason that people like Bill Gates, Steve Jobs, Jeff Bezos, Mark Zuckerberg and others spent many hours working on their inventions or businesses with urgent commitment and zeal as if they would not get another chance at whatever they were doing.

The importance of time for success and the creation of wealth is closely related to the concept of Time Value of Money (TVM). Investors hold the view that the sooner they make a dollar, the better off they are because they can then invest it to make more money. Similarly, when it comes to achieving success in general, the sooner you can achieve your goals, the faster you will achieve your purpose or goal, which in turn enable you to entrench your success.

Time is a commodity which anyone who is hoping to achieve success cannot afford to waste. Respect and value time for success. Generally, people who waste time do not achieve much of what they aspire to do. As you learn the value of time, you should also get rid of those who waste your time because they will get in the way of you reaching your destiny. Here is what respecting time will do for you:

- Prevent postponing and procrastination: Once you are conscious to the fact that time is money, you will use the time wisely and to do things promptly without delay.

- Make you more effective and productive: Those who value time have a sense of urgency and tend to be more effective and productive because they know that the only time, they have to do whatever they are working on is the time they have designated it. They work faster and are more committed and focused because there may be no other opportunity to do it!

- Better health and wellbeing: Good time management enables you to distribute your tasks and assign time sufficiently to cover all aspects of your life. If you finish today's tasks, you will not have to miss a family lunch or stay late in office tomorrow. You will have enough time for everything thus negating stress and other health debilitating issues caused by poor time management.

There Is Enough Time for Success

There is enough time in a day for you to do everything you want to achieve success if you have everything well planned to help you make good use of it. Never say that you do not have enough time because those who have achieved success have the same time at their disposal as you do, there is no bonus time for successful people- they simply plan better and prioritize their tasks to give them an edge.

Be Mentally Flexible and Open Minded

Nobody is born with all the knowledge they require or use for success- it is all acquired and learned. You must be open minded enough to accept new ideas because it is the only way to develop new skills to help you on the path to success.

Do Not Limit Yourself

You can never truly realize your full potential or achieve any success unless you get rid of limiting beliefs and habits, the subconscious paradigms that have been embedded in your mind. Negative beliefs can limit your potential and prevent you from succeeding. The power of the mind is the gateway to wealth and must never be underestimated.

Get A Mentor

Get a successful mentor to guide you on the journey to making money and wealth and whom you can get advice from and study so that you can apply their teachings for your own success.

Invest in Yourself

Whether in skills, knowledge, information, better health, etc. you must invest in making yourself better wholeheartedly; otherwise, you will not have what is required to help you succeed. Invest your time and money to improve your skills and better your mindset. Every successful person has invested in themselves before they invest in other things.

Decide What You Want, Once Decided Do Not Doubt It

It is vital that you remember that you are dealing with the law of attraction and making requests through your thoughts; you must decide what you want and once you have settled for something, do not second-guess or doubt yourself.

Doubt is the genesis of bad negative thought that is the antithesis of creative thoughts that will lead you to success; be clear and definite for unwavering sends the wrong signals and attracts unwanted results.

Write Down Your Desires or Wants

When you want anything, it is important that you write it down on a piece of paper; putting your thoughts down on paper is the first step to ownership of what you want. By writing your desires down, you have taken the first step in turning your thoughts and mental images into reality- you have started creating!

With writing, always start off with gratitude, e.g. "I am thankful and delighted that the new car I want is already mine……." And always write in the present tense for you want it now, and the universe is giving it to you now.

Actively and Audibly Ask the Universe for It

Once you know what you want and have it down on paper, ask for it. There are many ways that people address this step of the law of attraction, and I believe that prayers are the most common way of asking. You can ask at any time; you do not have to shout it out but say it loud enough for the universe to hear you.

Let the universe know what you want, how you want it, in what quantity, etc. and while requesting for whatever it is that you want, believe it is yours and see it as yours. You can only be given what you ask for.

Believe That You Will Get It; Trust the Universe

Once you have asked for what you want, move on believing and trusting that you have got what you want.

Stop worrying about what you asked for and how you will get it- leave the how to the universe and concentrate on the core principles of belief, trust, and appreciation. Do not run around in your mind anticipating or seeking what you asked for and do not be in a hurry; exercise patience and do not lose hope or be upset if things do not start happening immediately.

Some asks have taken decades to be answered, everything by nature happens time. You should move on in your stride and let the universe do the worrying on your behalf.

Meditation and Visualization

By far, mental relaxation is the easiest and sure way to get mental serenity and clarity which are the precursors to attaining the right frame of mind for success.

You need to take up one of the many forms of meditation that can easily fit into your lifestyle, and that you are comfortable practicing. It is important to remember that not everyone can do any form of meditation; because of age, health conditions, size, etc.

For optimal mind relaxation and rejuvenation, it is recommended that you perform guided meditate for five to ten minutes at a time, in a setting that is quiet and devoid of distractions. Early morning or late-night meditation is appropriate because these are the times that your surroundings are likely to be serene.

Once your mind is serene and clear then you can move on to active visualization; create exact mental images of what you want and go to them every time you go into guided meditation. If you visualize something long enough it will manifest faster.

Pick your object of desire, choose it in your mind to exact details, e.g. a green 4-door Peugeot, visualize it every day and meditate upon it until the day the universe delivers it to you.

Own and Possess

Once you have asked for the job promotion or the new house you desire, you need to put yourself mentally as if you already have it and feel it.

This step is what we commonly refer to our faith; absolute belief in the abstract is what is required here, it is difficult, but it is possible if you train your mind to lead you there. This is the most important of all steps you will read here yet it is also the most elusive.

Smile even if you are not happy and your spirit will inevitably be lifted, and you feel better; use the same principle for all the bigger things you want, and they will come to you. The law starts working here, so you must own and possess what is yours in your mind before it manifests itself for your realization.

Gratitude; Be Thankful for Everything in Your Life

Gratitude is a key ingredient for success using the principles of the law of attraction; be grateful for what you had, for what you have, for what you are asking for and for what you are going to have. You must be forever grateful for the blessings in your life whether material or immaterial.

Jot down the things you are thankful for and always remember to thank the universe for them; just like you and I are motivated by someone's show of gratitude in appreciation for what you have done for them, so is are the laws of nature. The law of attraction is heightened more when you appreciate what it gives you.

Giving gratitude for what you have and what you have accomplished sets the foundation for a positive attitude which enhances commitment. There is always something to be grateful for, however, small. Daily gratitude drives out feelings of failure and self-doubt which are often the catalysts of disengagement and a lack of commitment to our goals. Take a few minutes every day to appreciate your success which will cultivate in you a commitment and desire to succeed.

Think About It More and Think Positively

This is not a contradiction of what we discussed earlier, contrary to worrying; positive thought about what you want is greatly profitable to you. What you think about most is what you attract and what you become, therefore, what better things to think about than positive things you have asked the universe for.

Stop thinking about what you do not want or be bothered by the negative happenings of the past; negativity will beget your negativity.

Your Thoughts Cause Your Feelings and Your Feelings Attract

Having positive inner thoughts for positive and happy outer feelings is important for success; a positive mindset is seldom found in gloom. Your thoughts control your feelings, and that is why it is important that you cultivate, and nurture feel good thoughts and emotions for an upbeat attitude.

Mahatma Gandhi said that what you believe become what you think, your thoughts are your words, your words then become your actions, your actions turn to your habits, your habits become are your values and your values are your destiny.

Be happy, feel excited about life, be passionate about things, laugh, smile and the world will give you the same emotions and outcomes right back.

Begin to Talk About What You Want

Talk about what you want and 'have already got' with others and include them in your dreams. I would recommend sharing with positive people because they will help encourage you on the right path and remind you of the goal in cases where you stray off.

Speak in the undeterred knowledge and belief that what you want is a package in courier on the way to you.

Act Towards What You Want

If you do not work for success you cannot be successful; it is as simple as that. Do not expect that by deciding what you want, writing it down, and simply reclining in a shell and not doing anything is going to get you there—NO WAY.

There is no luck in getting what you want; even those who come by a windfall in the form of lotteries or any other such contests work to get it. Yes, they buy the tickets or take their time and register for the draws. Success is not a miracle, the right mindset is not a miracle, and the law of attraction is certainly not miraculous.

How Goals Help You with Success

Achieving success is only easy once it is done, the journey and certainly, the beginning is never easy. The goal setting process provides one indisputable guiding star for success which is clarity. Goals bring clarity to any action plan for pursuing and achieving any visions we want to realize; you create goals by defining the purpose first. When you have clarity, dealing with and surmounting challenges and obstacles becomes very easy because the objective is clear and set.

In whatever circumstance, if you want to ensure that you fulfill your potential and achieve success, you must have actionable and effective goals which are really the difference from what you dream about and what comes true. Success is not by accident; effective goals are a prerequisite:

Lead to Better Decisions
They help you to have a better understanding of what you are doing and working towards. Goals will slow you down so that you can make the right decisions and react appropriately to get what you want. Goals will help you align with the goals and put you in a comfortable place mentally to work for what you envision- you can better 'see' and consider more options for success. Goals help you to craft a plan for success.

Help You Understand Yourself Better
You can never succeed at anything if you cannot control your emotions to see thing clearly and goals will help you to translate your

feelings into action that are suited to your strengths and temperament. With clear goals, you will make your decisions, not what others want for you. Accept and interrogate your emotions and use them to guide you to success.

Goal setting enables clarity of purpose without which you will be bombarded with ideas, and you will be left drifting aimlessly doing one thing to another without achieving much.

Motivate You to Action

Goals are great motivators to get you pumped up and to work to achieve the vision you have. While motivation by itself will only get you so far, goals, which are essentially daily habits, will ignite the will and drive you to succeed. Wishing for things to happen will never take you where you want to be, only actions can get you the success you want.

Goals provide you with specific actions to take, which come together into an actionable plan for guiding you on what to do and at what point to do it. The real motivator is in knowing the benefits which await you when you meet every goal, which helps you to dig deeper and push through with the plan.

Bestow A Sense of Responsibility

A life without goals is a life without responsibility. Goals make you responsible for your success and the actions you take to get you there. Quite often, when we are not committed to something, we lack the compulsion and motivation needed to see it through. With goal setting, we are responsible for the outcomes we achieve in life and only have ourselves to blame or thank, and many times when we set goals, we realize success.

This will help you to push through. As you get closer to achieving your goal, you can see how far you've come, and you know that it would be a lot easier to keep going than to quit or turn back. The very act of putting your goal into words and getting started can be a great motivator.

Focus on The Trophy

The trophy here is the vision you have for yourself and want to attain. Since time is limited, having effective goals will help you to focus your energies on the things that really matter for your success by picking out what is important and reigning you in to concentrate on them. Goals help you focus on the specific tasks you have set out to do without being distracted or the temptation to postpone, as well as filtering out the extraneous things which do not add any value.

The most important thing to remember in goal setting for success is to never lose sight of your vision in the whole process. Success requires you to chase your dream fearlessly but within the set goals and the broader action plan. In the success equation, goal setting brings about the required focus and motivation and the necessary sense of purpose to help you realize your vision.

Now that you know what a goal is, what it constitutes and what is required to attain it, you are better equipped to get on the journey of goal setting mastery to apply the knowledge to achieve anything you want. All you must do is believe in yourself, make the necessary changes to get your plan moving and improve or even alter your mindset for success. Goal setting is the most important step to a positive mind and a more successful life personally, professionally and in business.

With the correct goal setting process, your goals are clearly defined, the first step to success which leaves you with a strong sense of achievement with every goal you reach and surpass. In the next chapter, we shall investigate the question of why most of us do not achieve the goals we set.

The foregoing millionaire hacks will get you to the right mindset for success. These principles can only work for you if you make them part of your daily life and routine; the same way you must drink water and eat daily is the same way you must use them daily.

Success is achieved by habituation; make these principles your habits to help you achieve the right mindset for success.

Chapter 13:
The Challenge

Throughout this book, you have learned what you need to help you take the right steps towards achieving a money wealth success mindset. The way to success is in the state of your mind—with the right mindset you can achieve any level of success that you desire. You should tirelessly strive to achieve a goal your goals by adapting the information in this book

Like every other skill, success requires learning and practice- you will meet challenges along the way and will make many mistakes as well, but with a good understanding of the process and a well-executed goal setting plan, success is guaranteed. The way to success is simple- do not stop, do not give up.

Importance of Belief

How do you trust wholeheartedly in the goal-setting process and in the attainment of your vision and purpose? Believing in the abstract is probably one of the most difficult steps if not the most difficult in this journey.

Paycheck to Paycheck to Millionaire

You know you want a new car to help you get to work more reliably, once you have the car you can put in more hours at work or even get a second job which translates to more income, when you earn more you will be able to buy the things you want or pay for your college etc. The challenge most of us face is the ability to reconcile the current situation and perceived reality with where they want to be or the reality they want to live.

We are doubters by nature, however, by employing a positive mindset and the law of attraction you initiate the emotional and mental conditioning to drive and work to get you what you want.

It is not for you to know everything, with time the answers will be made clear to you, and you will not only get clarity, but the way to get what you want will be shown to you. The way and the actions to take for you to get to your intended destination will be shown to you, and it will be up to you to notice and take advantage.

One of the powerful ways to exercise belief is to constantly have your goal playing in your mind trust that you will achieve it, create mental pictures of the actual and know that the way will be shown to you. It is like walking into your house at night and flicking the switch to turn on the lights; you 'KNOW' that by doing that the room you are walking into will be illuminated and I doubt that there is any one of us who ever doubts that the light will come on. In fact, we do not think about it- that is the same kind of belief that you need for this process to work for you.

You need to focus your attention on your vision and not your struggles or problems; let your vision lead you to where you want to go. Confidence and belief can only be created and owned by you; be confident and secure in yourself and have an inner abundance of positive thoughts, emotions, and visions for your life. The more positive you feel and believe, the more positive outcomes you are bound to get.

Do not seek anything from outside as all you need is within you; you are the creator of what you want. The universe is only giving you what you create on your own thus the need and importance of seeking within you first. Total belief in what you want and that you will get it is important to realize your desires, without it nothing will work for you. Start building confidence and belief by taking small steps towards total belief, and you will reap the benefits to transform your life beyond what you ever dreamed of.

You must stop worrying about how you will get what you want- that is not your job. Leave the how to the universe and concentrate on the core principles of belief, trust, and appreciation; do not overrun your mind anticipating or seeking what you requested.

Of course, you should not buy into blind belief; your confidence in getting what you want must be accompanied by actions aimed at reaching the desired goal. You cannot pray and sit on your laurels hoping for things to happen miraculously- it is for you to work and create the life that you want

Have unwavering belief in your dreams and in your ability to get them, and you will transform your life like a sculptor working away the unwanted bits to remain with the image he or she wants. So, how do you build the requisite faith to create the harmony you want in your life?

Belief or trust must be fed and nurtured to be able to get the potency and foothold desired; the best way to feed and grow your faith is through meditation and visualization.

Be focused, be positive, and follow a solid routine. Do not let your mind conjure negative images or harbor defeatist beliefs. Instead, teach it to focus on the current moment and on your current goals. Remember, success is about focusing on your present and giving your all to make it better. So, if you're really looking to be successful, be committed, seek knowledge, and make your journey enjoyable.

Nothing about being successful is instantaneous. And this is exactly why you can't expect an overnight change. In order to truly make things work in your favor, you will have to be strong, growth-oriented, and patient. While this might seem like a difficult and infinite journey, in the beginning, it is not quite the case.

Once you start following the advice in this book guidelines, every new habit you learn will become a part of your success-driven lifestyle. Good luck!

If you find this book helpful in anyway a review to support my endeavors is much appreciated.

How To

Achieve Finical Freedom, Success, and Prosperity. Quit the 9 to 5. Work 4 Hours a Week. Obtain Wealth and Money. Create Over 7 Highly Effective Habits to Do All of This

Chapter 1:
Habits

We all desire the best things in life—we want to have better financial status, form healthy relationships, live healthy lifestyle, and accomplish those goals that we've set for ourselves. Heck! These desires—or should I say, thirsts—are the main reason why we keep trying. It is the reason why we all study frequently, go to work, and why we build relationships. We want to spend our retirement days in a dream house with no outstanding mortgage payments, visit any choice vacation destination, and secure the future of our loved ones. Sadly, not everyone gets to accomplish that dream. For many of us, these dreams and desires get shrouded up in the frustrations and forgotten in the course of our life. Then, we ask ourselves, "what am I doing wrong?" whenever we have a brief awakening. We see others taking giant strides with perceived ease toward their goals. Our social media feeds are filled with these people's accomplishments; from posting about their new house to posting pictures about their exotic vacations. "Life just seems easy for these set of people," we say to ourselves. Unconsciously, we tend to sink back into ourselves and strengthen our old habits. Hold on! Did I mention "habits"? Yes, habits are the reason why success, wealth, and money have become an illusion to so many people. More so, it is the reason why some people are so successful at what they do. Let's look at why habits are so crucial to our dreams, goals, and personal development.

Why Habits Are Important

We all want a better future for ourselves. However, we often fail to regard the one thing that can bring this future to reality: our habits. Every action you take, no matter how small, can kickstart a chain reaction throughout your life. Yes, we forget that our habits can either make or mark us. A simple decision to exercise for 30 minutes a day can improve your health and influence what you're eating.

What's more? Cultivating the habit of having a family dinner can impact the psychological growth of your kids and boost your relationship with your partner. Smoking a cigarette every day can hurt your lungs and overall health. Yes, our life outcome is a result of our habits. Sadly, we all underestimate the power of our habits. We rarely pay attention to actions. Even when we do focus on our actions, we tend to overlook the inane and small ones. We convince ourselves many times that success requires a grandiose action. Whether it involves losing weight, winning a business deal or writing a book, we put pressure on ourselves to make an earth-shattering improvement that will make us famous.

Well, You Are Wrong.

The small habits matter. How? Let's observe the rule of compound interest in finance. Say you save $100 in an investment account with an interest rate of 10% per year; you will get an additional $10 on your initial deposit of $100 after one year. Now, you have $110. The subsequent interest payment will be 10% of your total sum, which is now $121. By the 5th year, your total amount would be approximately $193. This interest keeps compounding until you end up with a huge sum when you want to withdraw.

Small habits work in that same manner. Let's say you decide to invest 5 minutes of your time to exercise. It is impossible for you to notice any new change during the first few days. You may not see a change in the first few days of the second week of your newfound habit; you will only notice a slight change in the first three weeks. During this early phase of your new habit, it is easy to get discouraged since the effects are slow. I refer to this phase as the lag phase. It is the time when most people are tempted to slide back into old habits. If you, however, persist in your actions, the changes will slowly compound until it gains momentum, and this is the time other people will notice the change in you.

Conversely, a few negative habits can stall your growth and self-development. A few extra hours more in front of a TV; a few more hours to nap; and a few soft drinks can compound into an unhealthy lifestyle. Consequently, these unhealthy changes can either result in depression due to your inability to fulfill your goals, or it could result in a plethora of health complications.

That said, your success is not dependent on once-in-a-lifetime achievements; it relies on your ability to adhere to the positive habits in your daily activities. More so, if you want to predict the trajectory of your life, take a moment to observe the little positive and negative habits in you. Remember, time is the multiplier, and it will multiply whatever you invest in it.

Why It's Difficult to Adopt New Habits

Most of us are familiar with the success stories of a lot of popular figures. We know that Warren Buffet, the investment guru, started investment at an early age. What's more? Some are familiar with the story of how Thomas Edison was able to invent the light bulb after a myriad of trials. I know you can recollect word-for-word these success stories from books, TVs, and even the internet. There are so many books about success and the success stories of famous people; these books offer us a glimpse into the lives, habits, and strategies of those who are successful in their respective niche. Despite the wealth of information, we glean from these success stories and often find it difficult to adopt these same positive habits. More so, we find it difficult to break our habits to make room for new ones to grow. Bad habits are like oak trees that have taken time to entrench themselves into your core. Therefore, you need to find a way to uproot these habits, and this requires targeting keynote or foundational habits.

How To

Cast Away the Chains of Procrastination

Procrastination is a keynote habit you must break if you want to achieve your dream. According to Brian Tracy, the author of Eat That Frog, procrastination is the thief of time. It gradually lets you postpone important things until it's nearly too late for you to take charge or complete the task. Procrastination lies as one of the roots of all our bad habits. By procrastinating on curbing unhealthy eating habits or exercising, you are inadvertently compounding your health issues. By procrastinating on a business deal or investment, you are unconsciously drawing nearer to financial ruin. Let me ask you this question: how many times have you procrastinated on a task only to never do it again? It might be a quick errand or a simple task, such as flossing or airing the sheets. It is easier to procrastinate on tasks we perceive as unimportant, and this subsequently leads to failure.

The Illusion of Overnight Success

Just as you must break the chains of procrastination, you need to wake up from the illusions of overnight success. This illusion is sold by the media, your social media feeds, and con men. These outlets focus on the grandiose moments of an individual's accomplishments without care for the years of struggles, pain, discipline, and disappointment before they could achieve that dream. Sadly, some people are swayed by these grandeur moments. Also, we throw away our inhibitions and run after these illusions painted by the media. So, let me set the facts straight: there's no shortcut to achieving your dreams. Just as a child must crawl before it can walk and later talk, growth and development are in sequential order, and there's no alternative to this process. You must put in the hard work and persist even when the odds are no longer on your side. Funny enough, the logical part of your brain understands that the process of growth cannot be skipped. However, the emotional part of the brain finds it difficult to comprehend the concept.

Consequently, we could opt for quick ways to bypass the long process of growth and development. It is the reason why we easily fall into get-rich-quick schemes. Thomas Edison didn't become a well-recognized figure overnight; he reportedly failed so many times before he could invent the light bulb. Mahatma Karamchand Gandhi didn't achieve his dream for independence overnight; he went on numerous hunger strikes, walked for miles, and suffered a lot of persecutions before he achieved his breakthrough. So, look beyond the illusion of overnight success and peer into the backstage to get a glimpse of to achieve that change.

How to Create Long-Term Changes?
We adopt new habits because we desire to create lasting change in an area of our life. However, it's disappointing when we fail to adhere to these new habits due to a busy schedule or family emergencies or any other circumstances. Most times, we fail to adhere to these new habits because our reasons are weak. Therefore, I will show you how to adhere to these habits by incorporating the three main principles

of change into your daily activities. But hold on! Before we delve into these principles, I want to explore the importance of a paradigm shift and how it can help you to create lasting change.

Understanding Paradigm Shifts

Your paradigm or perception is the way you view the world. Surprising as it might seem, the way you view the world determines your success. It determines your good or bad habits. Just a slight shift in your perception can set the groundwork for your newfound habits. To understand this concept better, let's think of paradigms, or perceptions, like a map. The concept of paradigm is like maps. Just like maps, you will arrive at your destination if you have the right perception. Alternatively, having the wrong perception is just like having the wrong map: you will never arrive at your destination. You might have the right attitude or work faster and diligently, but you will still be lost if you have the wrong perception.

How Do We Form Paradigm Shifts?

Everyone has a literal map or perception in their head. Sometimes, these perceptions are based on reality, while some are based on values or the way we think things should be. These maps or perception becomes the lens through which we view and interpret all our experiences. We seldom question the accuracy of our perceptions. Heck! We rarely even notice their existence. We assume that things are the way we see them. More so, our attitudes and behaviors stem from these assumptions. Therefore, when we open our mouth to describe the things we see, we are inadvertently describing ourselves, our paradigms, and perceptions.

Why Some Never Have A Paradigm Shift

Most times, we are intrigued by the success and accomplishment of others. We admire their principles, teamwork, strength, maturity, and family bond. Some, however, take it a step further by requesting for the secret of their happiness, success, and techniques. Sadly, most of those who make this appeal are looking for a quick fix. Even taught these skills, they never really understand the depth and eventually lose it. It's the reason why some are rooted in the same position, despite reading a myriad of motivational books. Why? Because they are looking for a quick solution to their life issues without attacking the underlying problem of their stagnation.

The Power of an "Aha Moment"

Do you see the light bulb that shines above a cartoon character when it has an idea? Well, this is what happens when you have a paradigm shift or an "Aha Moment." This moment is what you experience when you start to see the world in a different light. It's a rare dose of epiphany that some people might not experience in their lifetime. At that moment, you become awed by the magnitude of another perception and how much you've missed out. Archimedes, a Greek mathematician, was able to create the floatation principle that is widely used in various aspects of engineering. His "Aha Moment" occurred when he went to take a soak at the public bath. He noticed that his body

How To

displaced part of the water in the tub as he stepped in it and that was the moment, he had his epiphany. So many prominent people today were able to create lasting habits through a paradigm brought about by an "Aha Moment."

Mind you, having a paradigm shift is not limited to an "Aha Moment." Sometimes, you get a paradigm shift in the face of life-altering experiences such as the death of a loved one, or at the top of taking a drastic step. Furthermore, your paradigm shift can come slowly as a result of a series of events that changed your perception.

THE THREE MAIN PRINCIPLES OF CREATING LASTING CHANGE

Raise Your Standards

It is sad that we underestimate our capabilities and demand so little of ourselves. Therefore, if you want to stand shoulder-to-shoulder with the giants you so much adore, you need to raise your standards. It's that straightforward. Write down the things you will no longer tolerate in your life and all the things you aspire to become. Put it up on the door of your room and your refrigerator. If, however, you find yourself doubting your capabilities, look at the lives of those who have made their marks in the world. From Martin Luther King Jr. to Rosa Parks, to Mahatma Gandhi, to Abraham Lincoln; these people changed the status quo, and history will never forget their impact.

Build Your Conviction

It is not enough to raise your standards if you don't believe in what you are doing. You had already sabotaged yourself before you started the habit. It's no surprise that many people are unable to follow a habit since they don't believe in the long-term benefit. Your convictions are like unquestioned orders, telling us what's possible and what's not possible, telling of how things are, and what we can do or not. They shape our actions, thoughts, and every emotion that we pass through. Therefore, building your conviction can raise your confidence and boost the confidence of those around you. Mind you, I'm not saying the process will be easy, but you can build your conviction via the following steps:

- Stop the negative talk: Never, I repeat, never practice self-criticism. Yes, we are our worst critics, but you should try to start trusting yourself and what you are saying. More so, avoid those who will sap your self-esteem with destructive criticism and negative talk.

- Reflect on your past achievement: It is easy to get weighed down by present circumstances. Therefore, try to reflect on what you have internally (self-worth; values; beliefs; love; compassion; confidence; happiness; experience; relationship; self-respect). Also, you can reflect on what you have externally (family; friends; career and business).

- Lastly, develop your convictions until you are firmly rooted in your beliefs. Remember, don't think about what others think of you, as this might be a stumbling block to your progress.

Change Your Strategy

When you raise your standards and build your convictions, I believe it's time to figure out a strategy to accomplish your goals. You have your goals in mind; you want to shed off some pounds; you want to have a million dollars at the end of a set duration. The next thing is for you to plan strategies to make your goals come to life. For you to accomplish this, you need to gain control over the five main aspects of your life: emotions, relationship, finance, time, and health.

Gain Control Over Your Emotions

Every action we take is basically to change the way we feel. For instance, you lose some extra pounds because you want to feel positive and confident about your body. Yes, we let our emotions drive our goals, and thus lead to various implications. When you depend on your emotions to make certain life-altering decisions, you will certainly make lots of mistakes. Failing to take control of your emotions can leave you at the mercy of outside elements.

Furthermore, you will never achieve your goals. Therefore, learning to control your emotions is an effective strategy to change your life. This time, you need to identify your overpowering emotions and how to use them to your advantage.

Gain Control Over Your Physical Health

You can never enjoy your accomplishments if you are riddled with poor health. It translates to failure if you ignore your health while building other aspects of your life. Learning to gain control over your physical health will help you to control your eating habits. Furthermore, it will help you to always go for medical check-ups. Remember, when you have good health that you can chase your goals.

Gain Control Over Your Relationships

Personally, there's nothing I can think of as important as gaining control over your relationships—family, business, social, and business. Gaining control over your relationships is a good strategy for creating lasting change. So, start by discovering what you value most, your expectations, your rules in the game of life, and how it relates to those around you. When you relate with those around you, you will be rewarded with a sense of contribution. More so, it will give the feeling that you've made a difference in other people's lives.

Gain Control Over Your Finances

According to recent studies, most American senior citizens are in financial constraints. Sadly, none of these people planned for this type of future as they worked toward their retirement. Therefore, you need to gain control of your finances right now irrespective of your age, status, or race. First, change the belief that money is the solution to an easier life or happiness. Rather, I want you to gain control of your finances, irrespective of the amount you have with you. The only way you can achieve this is by adopting new habits that will help you save toward your financial dreams. Let go of unnecessary expenses and build a future for yourself.

Gain Control Over Time

Time is not your friend. Time waits for no one. These are the basic misconception about money that we hear every day. Let me ask you a question: do you know how to use time? Permit me to change your belief right now: time is what you make of it. Let me explain further: if you decide to waste your time on instant gratification, then time will never be enough for you to chase your dreams. However, if you decide to manage your desires for instant gratification and allow your dreams and creations to grow, then time will become your ally. Once you finally gain control over time, you will find out that you can achieve so much within even a few days!

Chapter 2:
Start Your Day Right

We wake up every day to a plethora of tasks with varying magnitude and difficulty. Sometimes, we get discouraged to even start at all due to the enormity of what we must do. Why? It's because our mind automatically focuses on the big tasks while shifting the small tasks to the bottom of the list. We think if we can complete the big tasks, then we'll have enough time and motivation to jump on the less important ones. However, we find ourselves completely exhausted physically and emotionally after completing the bigger tasks. Sadly, we never get around to doing it until it overwhelms us. Little tasks such as making the bed can overwhelm you when done at the wrong time. In this chapter, we will look at the importance of each small task on our goals and dreams. Furthermore, we will examine the common misconception of completing small tasks, how to find your productive hours, and how you can establish your foundation habits. Before we do, let's discuss the bed-laying principle.

The Bed-Laying Principle
Admiral William H. McRaven, an alumnus of the University of Texas, was the keynote speaker at the University's 2014 graduation

ceremony. In a hall brimming with graduates eager for a taste of the outside world, the Admiral was able to deliver a stunning speech which, I believe, made an indelible mark on those present. After a brief introduction about his entry into a navy school, McRaven talked about the inspection procedure of his instructors at the academy. The instructors, who were veterans from the Vietnam War, would parade down the halls and inspect the recruit's beds. McRaven noted that no matter how much they laid their beds; the instructors just weren't satisfied. I find it surprising that these war veterans could focus on a small and inane task as bed laying. Could there be something more attached to it?

As if he could read my thought, the Admiral laid bare the bed-laying principle. He said start your day by changing the bed if you want to conquer the world. Laying your bed is an activity that counts as a small win and gives you the needed euphoria to take on huge tasks later in the day.

He also pointed out the fact that how are you going to complete the big tasks if you can't handle the small ones.

It Starts with The Small Wins

Just as Admiral McRaven graciously pointed out, simple habits or actions such as laying the bed are small wins that eventually give you the motivation to take on huge tasks. Various researches allude to the fact that these small or inconsequential actions can fuel transformative changes that become a pattern. Furthermore, the patterns formed convince you that bigger achievements are within reach. For instance, deciding to drink a glass of juice every morning can create a pattern for a healthy lifestyle.

What's more? This small habit will gradually become a pattern, and consequently, give you the energy to take on a huge task. However, not all small tasks are worth investing in. Some folks make the mistake of investing in small actions that have no positive impact on their ability to tackle huge tasks. For instance, small actions such as leaving dirty dishes in the sick to dedicate a few minutes to appreciate your loved ones can eventually become a pattern which will strengthen your relationships. Taking a minute to appreciate people will make you feel happy about yourself. And that is the reaction/emotion which will provide you with the needed motivation to tackle any task head-on.

Wait!

Before you jump on the bandwagon of doing any small habit, I want you first to identify the ones that will have a positive impact on you. What's more? I want you to select small habits that will kickstart a chain reaction of productivity in your life. Yes, there's a name for these types of habits, and they are referred to as keystone or foundation habits.

Harnessing the Power of Keystone Habits

How To

According to the bed-laying principle, some tasks have the potential to start a chain reaction, thereby influencing other tasks in your schedule. A simple task such as washing the dishes or vacuuming under the chairs can spur you to go on a cleaning spree in other parts of your house. With time, these minor tasks become habits or patterns which gradually seep into other areas. The power of keystone habits lies in the realization that you can get everything right; that you can't complete all the tasks in your schedule. More so, it lies in the ability to identify a few important priorities and fashioning them into powerful levers. I recommend starting with a small task with the potential of becoming a keystone habit. These tasks, however minute, will have the ability to shift and remake other habits. Here's an example to help you understand better. Paul wants to lose a few extra pounds to complete his company's annual marathon event. Since he became the vice president, there's no alternative for him; he must compete. The event is still three months away and every passing day fills him with the trepidation of losing. Rather than tremble at the thought of embarrassing himself on the D-day, Paul decided to act. He would wake up every morning by 5 a.m. to jog for 30 minutes. Paul thought he was going to die on the first day. The first few days were hell for him. However, the second and third week weren't that bad. With time, Paul noticed he had stopped eating more and become more conscious with his diet. Interestingly, he's more productive in his workplace. He has developed a great relationship with his colleagues. What's more? His family can't get enough of him. Now, what you think caused this chain reaction in Paul's life? The answer, my dear reader, lies in the power of keystone habits.

Here's another thought-provoking question: Why is it so difficult to adopt this concept since it seems so simple and easy? Well, the answer is not far-fetched. Heck! You might have said it yourself or heard it from those around you. Are you curious to know? Then, let's jump into the next section.

Statement 1: "I Don't Feel Motivated"

No doubt, this is one of the good old statements we use as an excuse when we fail to follow up on new habits. Don't deny it: we are all guilty of this at times. For example, we decide to change our lives, so we set a major goal and try to build habits to help us achieve our targets. We succeed for a few days until life throws a wrench into our newfound habits, thereby skipping a day. Sadly, the pattern repeats itself. We try again with a burning desire to push through irrespective of any circumstance. Once again, we miss a day or two dues to another circumstance which could be our old habits or external forces. Eventually, you quit in frustration and conclude that this is not for you. Do you want to know the truth? It's not easy building new habits, especially keynote habits. I'm sure many experts will tell you to cultivate a new habit by doing it daily. Yes, it's so easy to say those words or read them in a book. However, it is most difficult to see it through. Why? Because we live hectic lives, so it's difficult to try anything consistently. More so, it is challenging to add an extra task to your already tight and hectic schedule.

Motivation Is Not Enough; You Need Willpower

As you progress through life, you will realize that motivation is not enough—it's just the tip of the iceberg. Do you want to know what's beneath the iceberg? It's your willpower. Sure, you can listen to inspiring motivation talks or read books on success to get energized. However, motivation won't get you through the times when you're feeling tired and disenchanted about working on a task. Yes, this is the time when you need your willpower. Besides the possessing conscience, self-awareness, and imagination, your willpower is your fourth human endowment. It empowers your self-management strategies. It's the ability to make choices and decisions and act by them. The human willpower is an amazing concept that has helped so many people to surmount different situations. For examples, various studies prove that students with strong willpower had excellent grades compared to those without. These students spent less time in front of the TV or any distractions. Sadly, not everyone possesses strong willpower. Just like a muscle, you need to exercise your willpower continuously until it becomes strong enough to help you push through dire circumstances. So, how will you build your willpower? By practicing self-discipline. Self-discipline is derived from disciple, which means your ability to follow or stick to philosophy or habit. You need to stick to your small task's day-in and day-out until your willpower is strong enough.

Statement 2: "I Can't Remember to Complete the Small Tasks"

Here comes another common statement. This type of statement makes me ponder on the reasons why people fail to complete small tasks. After studying and interacting with so many people, I've come to one conclusion: the difficulty in completing small tasks is related to a concept called cognitive load.

Let me elaborate.

The human brain has a short-term memory and a long-term memory. We depend on our short-term memory when we try to accomplish and incorporate new habits. Sadly, the human brain can only store about seven chunks of information in its short-term memory. Since only a tiny fraction of what we know is stored in our working memory, we often depend on our long-term memory and habits to accomplish almost every task in life. For example, when you first learned how to drive a car, you had to put in a conscious effort to carry out the process for each action. This included tasks like parallel parking, changing lanes, driving with a stick shift, or using a turn signal. In the beginning, each of these tasks required a constant reinforcement of your short-term memory until it becomes a habit that does not require much thought process (long-term memory). More so, when it becomes a habit, it frees your mind to focus on other tasks, such as an off-key version to your favorite playlist.

Let's use a different example to demonstrate your cognitive load. Small habits such as tracking your expenses or doing your tax calculations are the key to gaining control over your finances. It is not hard to perform these tasks because they only require a few minutes to complete. However, it is also easy to forget because it's not an automatic component of our daily routine. Therefore, if you don't use a "trigger" to remind you of these small tasks, then it will be difficult for tracking your expenses daily. This is also the reason why it's easy to consistently perform simple tasks, such as brushing your teeth or bathing. Why? It is because you know the negative consequences of not brushing your teeth, and this acts as a trigger to spur you on.

Another reason why people often remember to perform consistent small tasks such as brushing the teeth is that it's attached to a larger routine that you complete when you wake in the morning. Therefore, brushing your teeth is an automatic action since it doesn't strain your cognitive load.

How Can You Adopt New Tasks?

So, how can you integrate new small tasks into your long-term memory to become automatic? Well, you have already discovered the answer yourself. You need to anchor or attach your new habits to an existing routine; or better yet, set a timer that notifies you of your tasks every day. There are myriads of ways with which you can carry out the small tasks in your routine.

Build A Priority List

Yes, it's that simple. Build a list of all your important activities and start with the small tasks at the top and the big tasks at the bottom. Arrange your small tasks and big tasks in order of importance or urgency. While making this list, you will realize that not all tasks are urgent or important. Furthermore, some task requires just a few minutes and little-expended energy, while others might gulp all your time and energy. So, I'll advise you to start with the ones that require less energy and less time before attempting the more tasking ones.

Declutter Your Daily Schedule

Why do you have to wear yourself out by attempting so many tasks in a day? Doing this will not only wear you out but fill you with a sense of accomplishment. In such a scenario, I want you to sieve through myriads of daily activities and select the ones with the potential to create a positive impact. Be realistic: you are not helping anyone if you wear yourself out. It might even affect your productivity for the next day.

No doubt, we often forget about the importance of each day in how our lives turn out. It is possible to overlook the little actions and big actions that sum up our day.

Chapter 3:
Life is Unfair, Get Over It

Life is unfair. Life is unfair to the employee who worked so much for a promotion but was bypassed due to his/her gender. Yes, it is unfair to the child born with cystic fibrosis, who might never have a fair chance at life. Let's not forget the war veteran who must live on scraps despite going on several tours for his country. Life is unfair to the woman who had to suffer emotional abuse at the hands of her loved one. Have you forgotten about life's unfairness to a student who was denied a scholarship based on the color of his skin, despite exceeding the requirements? What about the child who had to grow up in an abusive environment? Do you want to know the truth? Life is unfair to everyone. No matter what, life will never give you only rainbows and unicorns; you will also get to taste the wrong side of life. Everywhere you go, you see people blaming their loved ones, their friends, their country, even the world. Do you want the bigger truth? Life is what you make of it. Perhaps, you think you have the worst situation in the world, and no one can ever grasp the depth of your situation. Well, here's an example to show you someone who had it worse.

Jeremy Napier

Life Is What You Make of It

Jake and Mark are twin brothers. They lived in the makeshift home made from wood and pieces of cardboard to shut out the elements. All their lives, they've neither felt the warm embrace of their parents nor do they know affection. They lost their parents and elder siblings at an early age to the greedy hands of death due to an epidemic that swept across the village. Life was difficult for these twins in an area with little-to-no resources. They had to scrounge from the leftover bones at the butcher shops and rummage through the refuse heaps to find a few good vegetables. No one ever thought to lend a helping hand. Why? The villagers all felt they were unfortunate and didn't want their aura to cross their doorstep. No one wanted them around, even little kids who are often known to have no fear of strangers, steered clear of the twins. Life would, however, offer them a reprieve in the form of a vacancy for workers on a construction site. Now, let's fast forward to the future: Jake is married with three beautiful kids and a happy and healthy circle of friends. Also, he's the regional manager of a large store in the city. Mark, however, is a chronic alcoholic, drug addict, and financially broke. He's back in the makeshift home of his childhood. Interestingly, both men turned out differently despite growing up in the same restrictive environment.

Let me ask you: what could have gone wrong?

Perhaps, we should ask both men the reason why they are in their present predicament?

How To

Do you know what they will say?

Interestingly, both men would say, "What could I have become, having grown up in that deplorable condition." Well, they couldn't have been far from the truth. So many times, we have been seduced to think that our environment shaped us the way we are, and events control our thoughts. And this is the greatest lie of all because life is what we make of it. If you believe that you are a victim of your circumstances, then you become a victim. On the other hand, if you believe that you can make the best of your life despite the glaring disadvantage you've been served, then you will achieve your goals. Our beliefs, rather than our circumstances, have the power to shape us.

What Is Belief?

It is necessary for us to start with a simple introduction before I explore the complex aspects of how beliefs influence our perception of the world. So, what are beliefs, anyway? Beliefs are feelings of certainty about something. For instance, if you believe that you are beautiful, what you are trying to say is, "I'm certain I'm beautiful." That sense of certainty allows you to tap into innate resources that prove you are beautiful - it's that simple. Interestingly, we all have the potential for virtually anything. However, we limit ourselves via our lack of certainty in belief.

Here's another way to understand the concept of beliefs: beliefs are made up of tiny building blocks called ideas. There are lots of ideas running through your head right now. However, you don't believe all of them. An idea can only become a belief when you are certain of its authenticity via your inner convictions or from external forces. Here's a way to differentiate a belief from an idea. Stop for a few minutes and say to yourself, "I'm brave." Now, how certain do you feel about that statement? Well, if you think, "perhaps, I'm not brave," you are not certain of your courage.

Alternatively, if you believe that you are brave, then you might experience some references from those around you. For instance, people may have commended you quite a lot about your braveness. However, all these commendations mean nothing until you have solidified the belief in your heart.

Beliefs Are Formed Through Generalization
Beliefs are often the guiding force which tells us what will lead to pain or pleasure. For instance, when something happens to you, the brain asks two questions: "Will this lead to pleasure or pain?" and "what must I do avoid pleasure or pain?" The answer to these questions relies on our beliefs and we form beliefs through generalization. Generalization directs all our actions and determines the direction and quality of our lives. These generalizations help to simplify our lives. For instance, what allows you to drive a car? You sit in the driver's seat and stare at the steering wheel, gear, and ignition, and it becomes familiar to you even when the car model is different. Your

experience of driving a car gives you creates a sense of generalization when it comes to driving other cars.

Your Beliefs Have the Power to Build or Destroy

I want you to know something right now: it is never the events of your life, nor is it your environment. However, the meaning and interpretation you attach to the events are what shapes you into who you are. Beliefs are the difference between a hero and a villain; the haves and the have-nots. It's the difference between those that are happy and unhappy. For example, have you ever noticed how people gravitate toward you when you feel happy within yourself? It's almost as if you have a brilliant sun shining within you. Conversely, when you feel gloomy, it's almost as if people shy away from you.

Your beliefs can influence your external environment and bend them to your will. More so, we all can take any experience, beautiful or not, and create a meaning that can either save our lives or destroy it. There are people who have passed through traumatic experiences such as rape or abuse. Instead of letting these bad moments define them, they took the stand to protect those who must pass through the same moments. Some lose their loved ones to devastating illness and created shelters to protect those who are suffering from diseases. That, I believe, is their way of creating lemonade out of the lemon life has so graciously offered to them.

Everyone can tap into those bad situations and channel them into positive endeavors to become better. Sadly, many people never get to tap into it. Many people don't even recognize their bad beliefs. If you don't adopt the faith that there's a reason for all the tragedies in life, then you will never truly live. Always look for the silver lining. I know life doesn't always turn out the way you want due to circumstances beyond your control. But you can determine the lessons you want to learn from these experiences. Some Holocaust victims were able to survive because they chose not to determine their lives by the action of those soldiers.

Even in psychology, beliefs can cause biochemical changes in the body. Several studies in multi-personality disorders show that the potency of belief of these patients' belief they have become a new person, resulted in massive changes in their biochemistry. There are several studies that documents the patient's eyes changing as they assume a new identity. Even diseases, such as high blood pressure and diabetes, appear and disappear in tandem to the person's belief as to which identity they're impersonating.

It is common for some to develop the "life is unfair" mentality. These people develop a limiting set of beliefs about who they are and what they are capable of. Because they've experienced failure multiple times, they believe they won't be able to succeed in the future. More so, they tend to focus on being "realistic" out of fear of failure and pain. People who often say, "life is unfair" or "let's be realistic" are afraid of being hurt again. They also restrain themselves from going all out on a project because they think failure is a constant in their lives. Sadly, it is the same reason why sets of realistic people will rarely get to the top of their niche. Leaders, on the other hand, are rarely realistic. They are intelligent and are not realistic by other people's standards.

The Danger of Looking Through the Social Mirror

The world will always find a way to give you a label. Sadly, most people let themselves be defined by these labels. More so, it becomes so limiting that we accept it as our truth. How many times have you let people decide what you are, what you can do without having a say in it? Once, twice, perhaps all your life? Sadly, most people base their beliefs in life on the current social paradigm, based on people's perception and opinion about them. Here's a question for you: have you ever looked at your reflection through those disjointed mirrors at a carnival? Do you get a perfect reflection of yourself? Hell no!

People would say, "you are crazy," "you will never amount to anything," "you eat like a pig," "why are you so dull?" etc.

Perhaps, you might come across a plethora of such paradigms from people. However, just like disjointed mirrors in a carnival, people's opinions are not a true reflection of whom and what you are. It is often a projection of the character and weakness of people giving the input.

Sometimes, social paradigms claim that we are largely determined by the conditions. Furthermore, these social paradigms postulate that we have no control over the circumstances of our lives. Yes, we all agree that these social paradigms influence our decisions. However, they do not control our lives. To back up these claims, society has created three social maps to explain the nature of man. Sadly, these social maps are accepted globally.

The 3 Social Maps

Genetic determinism is another way of society telling us that some of our circumstances are created by our grandparents. They try to tell you that you inherited your fiery temper from your grandparents. In other words, they say it's in your DNA. It goes from generation to generation.

Psychic determinism, also described as the Freudian psychology, is the social map that says your parents did it to you. Your childhood experience and your upbringing will lay out your tendencies and character structure. They explain everything based on how you were brought up. For example, if you are afraid to speak in front of a crowd or feel self-conscious whenever you do something in front of people, some will say it is because you were castigated and emotionally brutalized when you were a kid. This is a common example of psychic determinism.

How To

Emotional determinism says that your life is a product of your environment and those who surround you. It says your boss, wife, your nation, the economic situation, and circle of friends are the reason for your present condition. Going back to the example of Jake and Mark, we cannot deny that the environment influences their decision. However, Jake was able to rise above the environmental determinism; he was able to transform his environmental paradigm into the fuel for his success. Conversely, Mark was satisfied with the environmental determinism.

Each of these maps is based on the concept that we are conditioned to react in a certain way to a specific stimulus. Failure to break from these limiting beliefs can lead to depression and unhappy life. You must be proactive.

Take the Initiative to Change Your Story: Become Proactive

Enough of the sad story: it is time to stop complaining about your circumstances. Rather, I want you to look at all things you think are unfair in your life. Picture them right now. Now, think of what you desire in your life; a promotion, a better job, a new house, more money, children, and a healthy lifestyle. Since you now have a clear picture of what you desire to change, I want you to imagine squashing those circumstances. Yes, bury them beneath your desire for a better life. This is about you are taking the initiative; to refuse to be defined by your circumstances. Realize that you are the architect of your life and make your dreams happen. Humans by nature are proactive. If

Jeremy Napier

your life is a function of your circumstance and condition, it is because you have chosen to empower those factors.

Furthermore, you become reactive to every external stimulus. Reactive people are affected by their physical and social environment. For example, if the weather is bad, they feel bad. However, proactive people carry their own ray of sunshine with them. They don't care if it rains or not; they feel indifferent. What's more? They are value driven.

Reactive people are susceptible to the social environment. As mentioned earlier they are reactive to people's opinion and perceptions about them. If people treat them well, they feel well. When they don't, they become protective or defensive. By depending on people emotionally, reactive people are allowing other people's weaknesses to control them.

Mind you, I'm not saying proactive people are immune to these external impulses. Rather, their response to the stimulus is entirely value-based.

Remember, no condition can control or determine your fate unless you allow it.

So, take the initiative. I'm not saying you should be aggressive, pushy, or obnoxious. It means recognizing your power to effect change. Take our time to study more, take more aptitude tests, read books, have more interest in your work, invest more in your family; these are the

How To

proactive tasks I want to you take. More so, I want you to do more. Your condition was never holding you back. Rather, you are the one holding on these circumstances as a crutch to defend your inactions. Want to become better? Be proactive Be responsible. The world is a place filled with fairy tales and reality, but it is never unfair!

Chapter 4:
Embrace the Hurdles in Life

The Boogeyman Is Back!

This time, he is not hiding in our closet or underneath the bed. He is no longer restricted to nighttime or our nightmares; rather, we see him in the light of the day. While growing up, we thought we were finally free of the boogeyman. However, we see it in all its ugliness and monstrosity; we see it when we wake up, on our way to our office. Sometimes we close our eyes to avoid looking at this monstrosity, but we still see it in our mind. Gradually, it wears us down as we ask ourselves, "what does it want with me?" Yet, we never looked it in the eye. We've never even asked about its mission. We prefer to huddle in fear as it blocks our path. Sadly, some might never face the boogeyman all their lives, while others are forced to face it.

The boogeyman in this example is the hurdles and obstacles we face daily. Unlike the boogeyman of our childhood fantasies, this is real, and the realization scares us to the bone. We all know that hurdles come in different forms and magnitude. Some challenges or hurdles might come in the form of financial barriers, where your dreams and aspirations are cut short due to insufficient funds. More so, it could be due to physical disadvantages. Also, it could be due to rising unemployment, a decayed educational experience system, an examination, and even a toxic relationship. Whatever these hurdles are, they all serve one purpose: to block our dreams and goals. Irrespective of your status or station in life, these obstacles are a constant. It is the main constant of human evolution, and it will still be there long after you are gone. When we, however, do face it, we are left with two choices: we either sit in a corner paralyzed by our fears of the obstacle, or we rise to the challenge and face it? So, I'm asking you: which would you rather choose, the former or the latter? Do you want to know your answer? You will choose the latter. Everyone would go for the latter. Why? It's because we all want to achieve our goals and we know the only way to do that is to embrace our hurdles. However, most people tend to dream and fantasize about their goals, without the thought of rising to the challenge. They prefer to watch in awe and celebrate those who rise above the same hurdles they are so scared of. More so, some go down a dark path by blaming their lives, relationships, jobs, environment, parents, and everything that surrounds them for their predicament. As mentioned in the previous chapter, it's time to stop looking at the world as if it's unfair. Rather, it's time to embrace the scary boogeyman. It's time for you to stop seeing it as your enemy

Acknowledge the Obstacles Before You

Jeremy Napier

Do you why we prefer to huddle in fear before our obstacles while fantasizing about a possible solution? It's because we let our obstacles define us and hold us back. Our physical height, weight, age, relationship, and even what people think about us, are some of the obstacles we face. No doubt, we all have faced unique obstacles, but have you taken a moment for those who came before you. History is overflowing with athletes who are considered too small for their niche, pilots with dreadful eyesight, racial disadvantaged people, school dropouts, dyslexics, and dreamers ahead of their time. Perhaps you've also come across stories of those who grew up in a worse environment, where their very existence was being threatened.

Here's a question for you: what happened to them? Well, many gave up along the way. But a few didn't. They practiced harder at overcoming their challenges. Their obstacles honed their skills in looking for weak spots and shortcuts. Yes, they were tossed around to the point where they nearly gave up. Do you know why and how they triumphed? They saw their obstacles as an opportunity. Hold on! They didn't stop at that; they took the step to do something special about it. These set of people give us hope. Their stories help cement the fact that it is impossible to surmount any obstacle. These stories show us they were able to achieve victory via a cocktail of creativity, daring, and focus. Want to know what's more surprising? These people never had access to the plethora of information you have at your disposal. Want to know more? Some were even born with zero chance of success.

Right now, I want to look at those things that stand in your way; look right at it and don't back away. Hold on! Don't blame it. Don't hate it. Rather, embrace it and see it as the passage to your next step. Funny, right? You may say, "I can embrace my disability or disadvantage." Yes, you can. History has proved it to us, and you can do it, too. Are you ready to explore the next phase? Then, let's see the first step you need to take in embracing your hurdles.

Harness the Discipline of Perception

Why do we keep coming back to this word: perception? It's because perception is the one concept that separates the successful from those who are not. It is simply the way you see the world. If you see it as a cold place filled with cheats and crooks, then you will come across those who exhibit that trait. What's more? Even if they aren't, your mind will still interpret according to your perception. John Rockefeller was one of those who saw the world differently: he saw it as a place filled with boundless opportunities. Throughout his lifetime, he never got flustered during chaotic events. Rather, he prospered and soared. He surely wasn't the most brilliant. Rather, he chose to learn from market crashes and depressions. In life, we will surely come across obstacles, but what matters is our reaction to it. And our reaction stems from our perception, which is the way we see the problem. Where one sees a crisis, another sees opportunity. Where some are blinded by the glamor and blitz of success, some see reality with ruthless objectivity. You must realize that every reaction and emotion you experience are functions of your perception.

I know it's not so easy.

Yes, we live in a different time and a gilded age. We have experienced two major economic crashes, exponential rates in unemployment, and a concurrent rise in housing costs. Global warming and erratic weather conditions plague our daily life.

These occurrences have a negative toll on people, and they breed negative emotions. However, the ball is in your court; you can decide to look beyond the outward appearances. Yes, you can learn to cut through the illusion of the problems that seem to overwhelm us. Discipline in perception is what you need to look beyond the illusion. This will help you to see the advantage and the proper course of action to take in the face of an obstacle. With this, you will never be a slave to your fears or impulses. You can achieve this by transforming that disadvantage into a fortune, skill set, or education. Here are a few tips to help you harness the discipline of perception.

Firstly, learn to be objective. Secondly, learn to keep your emotions at a keen level. Thirdly, steady your nerves and ignore what limits others. Furthermore, choose to see the good in all situations and focus on what you can control.

How To

Recognize Your Strength

I want you to know that you are never completely powerless. Even when it seems as if all is lost, we are still in control of our minds. The ball is in our court whether you are going to break or survive. The world can label you, call you handicap, poor or unfit, but it doesn't matter. Popular figures such as Malcolm X, Nelson Mandela, and so many others have come to understand this fundamental distinction. They were able to turn a prison into a workshop where they transformed themselves, and the education center where they could educate others. When you have your wits around, you can step back and realize that there's a silver lining to every situation. For instance, let's say an employee made a drastic mistake that cost you a fortune. I'm sure this is a situation you've spent so much time and effort to avoid. Instead of you being a lament about the loss, change your perspective. See this situation as an opportunity to break beyond the barrier and to rise.

Live in The Present

Do you want to know a secret? Many great corporations like Microsoft, LinkedIn, Hewlett-Packard, Charles Schwab, Walt Disney Company, and so many more, started operation during economic and stock market crashes. Surprising? When others are closing shop, these pioneers were creating companies. Why? Because the founders were busy living in the present. Surely, they didn't know if it will get better or worse, but they just knew what was going to work.

They knew they had a great idea, and they took steps to make it work. However, most people aren't content to deal with things as they happen. They prefer to trouble themselves with what is fair or not, what's behind this or that, and what others are doing. By the time they get worked up over inane things, they have little-to-no energy to deal with their problems. As explained in the previous chapter, most people start with a disadvantage, and they perform well. Why? Because they took things step-by-step.

Focus on the present and not the imaginary boogeyman that might be ahead or not. Rather, take every day one step at a time. It doesn't matter whether you are in a good or bad job market. It doesn't matter if this is the worst time to be alive. What matters is to embrace your obstacle by living in the moment. Moreover, the more you embrace your hurdles, the easier they become.

It's not enough to live in the moment—you must work at it. Discard distracting thoughts and catch your mind when it wanders off. As you do this, I want you to remember that this moment is not your life. Rather, it's just a moment in your life. Ignore why the problem is happening to you and focus on what's in front of you.

Get Moving

"Oh! It's not yet time; I'm still waiting for the right moment." "Perhaps, it's not my turn yet." These are the common excuses you will hear from those around you. Some might say, "I can't launch this business idea until I have a million dollars" or "I can't be happy until I have enough money to buy my dream house or visit my vacation destination." Let me ask you this: what would have happened to the racial discrimination in the States if Civil Rights activists like Martin Luther King Jr. and Rosa Parks said it wasn't time yet? People like Amelia Earhart weren't satisfied with just sitting in the sidelines in a profession dominated by men. Rather, she chose to defy the odds and break the stereotype. She didn't care that the world said it wasn't time for women. Instead, she took the step and became the first woman to fly solo across the transatlantic. This accomplishment wouldn't have occurred if she didn't take that step.

Most times, we know what our problems are. We may even know what to do about them. However, we fear that acting is too risky; that we are not experienced or capable enough.

Let me tell you the truth: the right moment will never come. So, I want you to tell yourself: the time for my excuses is over. The bell is rung, and it is time to start moving.

We often have the misconception that the world moves at our pace. So, we delay when we should initiate action. We tip-toe when we should be running and soaring above the skies. Then, we get surprised when the breakthrough never occurs. It is at this moment when the enemies can get their act together. While you are relaxing and thinking of a thousand reasons why you can't act, someone somewhere is building a plan that would put you out of business. This is not the time to get comfortable and to rest on your oars. Rather, it's the time to keep moving, even when the obstacle won't budge, and even when you get frustrated in the pursuit of your goals. It's time to walk the talk.

See the Education in Your Defeat

If you think that you can always move your obstacles on the first try, you are wrong. Sometimes, it takes repeated efforts and strategies to clear away the problem. This concept is why most startups in Silicon Valley succeeded. These startups don't launch a product with polished and completed features. Instead, they introduce their Minimum Viable Product (MVP), which is the most basic version of their product with minimal features into the market. The purpose of this concept is to gauge their customers' response. If the response is bad, they go back to the drawing board and improve the product based on their customers' feedback. These innovative individuals have changed their perception of obstacles.

They see failure or setback as an opportunity to improve their designs. It's no surprise that these startups are growing at an exponential rate. Therefore, it's time to see yourself as a startup; change the way you view failure. See it as part of your journey toward your destination. Every success story is preceded by scores of failures. These successful people that you read about today aren't ashamed of their failures. Rather, they saw the education in it and devised new ways to conquer it—it's that simple.

Yes, I know failure hurts. However, I'm sure we can all admit that temporary and anticipated failure hurts less than permanent or catastrophic failure. When you expect failure along your path, you will be better prepared to handle it when it occurs. When it comes, be glad to pay the cost and have the hope that this is not the end of your journey. However, if you fail to learn from your failures, you will watch as your dreams sift through your fingers like sand.

Take A Walk

Want to know a final secret to embrace your hurdles? Take a walk, exercise more, or do something that will take your mind off the magnitude of the challenge. Richard Branson, when asked about the secret to his productivity, said he exercises daily. It is vital to find a way to clear your head either via a walk or through exercises. More so, you can practice meditation to ease the stress of your daily routine; in fact, so many studies allude to the soothing benefits of exercising on the brain. Exercises fill you with a sense of euphoria—also commonly known as endorphins—which enables you to take on other tasks. More so, it helps gives you a clear perspective on the obstacle you are so scared of.

Chapter 5:
Uncomfortable Means Opportunity

Your hands are shaking as you hold the speech in your hands. It is almost time for you to climb up the lectern, and it feels as if you might pass out at any moment. Sweat droplets bead across your eyebrows and streak down your back. Even your armpits are not left out from this "waterfall." You tell yourself over and over that you can do it. Since you've practiced a lot before a mirror, this should be easy. Then, another thought crosses your mind, and you curse the day you accepted the task. Alas, it's your company's dinner party, and you've been chosen to represent your team to deliver a speech. From your position at the back of the hall, you can see the company's executives and other important dignitaries. Even your family members are around to cheer on. Oh no! The compere just called your name. As you walk toward the stage, it's as if your legs are filled with lead: every step is heavy and unbearable. You ask yourself, "How am I walking properly? What are they saying about me? Was that chuckle meant for me?" Before you know it, you are already on the stage. "Everyone is watching," you tell yourself in trepidation. At that moment, every quip you've lined up to break the ice is practically out the window.

How To

However, you decide to soldier on and deliver the speech as best you can. It was a shock when you were greeted by a standing ovation at the end of your speech. All through the dinner event, people couldn't stop talking about how brilliant you were on the stage. The executives keep stealing glances at you, while your team members are showering you with praise. However, you are still in a daze. As the euphoria of the experience wears off, you remember how scared you were before the speech. You remember how you decided to take on the task when others shied away from it. You've never done anything like that before.

You return to the office the next day, and your boss couldn't stop thanking you for making the team proud. Later that month, you have successfully represented the company in different capacities. Now, you have a new office to yourself with greater responsibility and higher pay. Then, you ask yourself one more time, "How did I get here?"

Yes, how did this individual move from grass to grace; from the back of the queue to the front. Well, it's simply because he sacrificed his comfort to break forth from his daily routine. He decided to step out of his normal routine; and at that moment, he cemented his fate. By leaving his comfort zone, he was able to accomplish what would take years in just a month. Most times, we fail to realize the abundance of potential within us because we fear the unknown. Without even trying, we just prefer to keep on living without a taste for more. And this is how we become stagnant.

Opportunities Lie Beyond Your Comfort Zone

Life is a great teacher, overflowing with so many opportunities waiting for us to grab them and to own them. However, most of us never see these opportunities. We deny their existence and claim that opportunities are just like kid's stories. So, why do we deny the existence of opportunities? Why is it so much easier to blame the system and everything wrong in it? Why do we fail to notice that those who have made their mark on history have passed through the same circumstance? More so, do you realize that most successful people have had it worse than you?

Yes, these are the questions that we need to answer. The main reason many fails to rise above their station in life is they are afraid to step outside their comfort zone, which is where opportunities reside. Technology has made everything so much easier. Today, people rarely walk to their destinations as there are a variety of means to make or easier for them. With just a click on an app, you can get an Uber ride to anywhere you want. There's no more hunting or foraging through the wild for food since we can get everything from our nearby mall. Most technology innovations are driven by a need to increase comfort levels. For instance, elevators take away the stress of climbing stairs. Hold on! I'm not complaining about the dishwasher or microwave—I'm not crazy. Yes, it's a natural human instinct to always seek pleasure and to avoid pain and discomfort. Most times, we succumb to these instincts and end up stunting our growth. We must understand that great things happen when we try to take a risk by delving into the unknown. Great things become sweeter when we go through discomfort to achieve them—it's that simple. We wouldn't value opportunities without the pain we passed through before we could attain them. For instance, you can't become a great speaker if you don't take the step to break out of your comfort zone. It's the reason why great speakers like Anthony Robbins are at the top of their niche. In his book, "Awakening the Giant Within," he talks about how he left his comfort zone by reading over 700 books in school. What's more? To become fluent and better at public speaking, he broke the barriers of his comfort zone by taking every speaking job he could get his hands. Within the space of a decade, this former janitor became one of the most celebrated speakers in the world today. What did he do? He stepped out of his comfort zone by embracing discomfort until he achieved his goal.

Comfort Is Overrated!

Every day, we endure the boring routine of our daily activities; we prefer to sit at that job we hate. Yes, we contend ourselves with the race of life in a bid to be comfortable. We forget that man was never meant to be comfortable always. Comfort was only meant for rejuvenation and nothing more. Comfort causes people to close their eyes for one second and find out that they've wasted 30 years. Comfort is what makes the overpaid CEO rest on his achievements, while someone is building the next product to put out of business. Yes, comfort, contentment—whatever you prefer to call it—is overrated. More so, people mistakenly associate it with happiness. We forget that happiness lies in the completion of a daunting task in our discomfort zone. If you asked the person in the illustration above, he would surely tell you he felt happy at the end of the speech. The promotion you've been waiting for lies at the end of that professional course you dread so much. Remember there's nothing wrong with a little discomfort. It's the necessary spice of life to reach your target.

When to Embrace Discomfort

Not every discomfort is worth embracing. You should know that there are different types of discomfort and there are certain situations where these discomforts are classified as helpful and not harmful. To understand this better, here's how to know if the discomfort is the right move for you.

1. Embrace Discomfort When It Feels Safe

Yes, you need to embrace discomfort to tap into potential opportunities. However, you need to practice caution. For instance, a first-time juggler shouldn't start with chainsaws or any other heavy machinery. I understand I'm trying to take you out of your comfort zone. However, it's not an excuse to be foolish. This section is important if you want to encourage yourself to keep stepping out of your comfort zone. It is more difficult to step out of your comfort zone if you immediately get hurt on your first try. This is the time when you must start small and incorporate the small habits, we talked about in the first chapter. You can't start exercising by running a thousand miles the first time. Rather, you start with a mile then you pick up the pace until you can finally reach your goal. Mind you, sometimes life unexpectedly throws us in extremely difficult zones. In this instance, you must ride through it without receding into your shell.

2. Embrace Discomfort When It's Repeatable

In other words, embrace discomfort when you can form a positive habit from it. Discomfort is useful when the situation can be repeated, and these subsequent repetitions will make it more comfortable for you. For instance, starting a new diet like Paleo or Keto is usually hard. To some, this is way into their discomfort zone. You will probably feel like dying in the first two weeks, especially when your body undergoes ketosis—a metabolic state where the body runs on fat instead of sugar. However, this new eating habit will gradually become easy for you to follow. However, if you scald your skin, you might learn a valuable lesson from it and become tougher from the experience, but you wouldn't want to experience it all the time. Why? Because the overall potential for growth via that incident is weak.

There's a clause to this: one-time ventures in discomfort zones can help change your perspective. Perhaps, it can give the "Aha" moment. For instance, some people say a single skydiving experience changed their perspective. Skydiving falls into the discomfort zone, and it's an opportunity to face your fears head-on. It will give you the courage to tackle other areas you fear.

3. Embrace Discomfort When There's A Clear Benefit
Public speaking is uncomfortable, but it boosts your confidence levels. Exercise and a good diet are uncomfortable, but they increase your overall health and fitness. Generally, the benefits of discomfort make you stronger either emotionally, physically, or mentally. So, if you strategically and intentionally expose yourself to difficulty, your body will become accustomed to it as you progress. Mind you, I'm not trying to glorify hardship. We have all experienced one or two things that we wouldn't want to experience again. However, this is to show you the type of discomfort you can introduce into your life.

Still find it difficult to embrace the uncomfortable. Then, you need to incorporate these habits into your daily schedule.

Deep Breathing
Have you ever had a panic attack where you feel as if the walls are closing in on you? The reason why you are hyperventilating is that you were exposed to a stressful situation. Although some of us might not suffer from a panic attack, we lose focus during these situations. Well, not to worry. According to recent studies, taking slow deep breaths can help keep you calm and collected. More so, it distracts you from the uncomfortable situation and helps you to feel at peace. Here's how to do the deep breathing exercise: inhale and count to 5, then

slowly exhale for about 7 seconds. How do you feel now? At that moment of completing the breathing exercise, the uncomfortable situation becomes less threatening to you.

A Few Seconds of Distraction Will Change the Scales

Most people see distraction as one of the obstacles to achieving their goals. Well, they are right. Too much of a distraction can derail you from your target. However, just a little dose of distraction is needed before you decide, especially when you feel uncomfortable. It's common practice for people to take a break in an office meeting, especially when people are becoming more uncomfortable. You can replicate this action by using a few minutes to help you gather your thoughts. You can focus on something you love to take your mind off the uncomfortable situation. This is the same principle doctors use when giving immunization shots to kids: they distract them from the task at hand by offering them a toy.

Be Kind to Yourself

I can't emphasize this enough. The world is already unfair as it is, you don't want to add to the baggage. No one is going to love you or understand you as much as you do. When faced with an uncomfortable situation, it's alright to feel scared. But don't ever criticize yourself. Here's a trick I use during this situation: I would imagine what I'd tell someone else passing through the same situation. I'll write it down and read it to myself—trust me, it works! Remember, be kind to yourself and find a way to use your emotions to fuel your actions toward opportunities.

Chapter 6:
Easy Offers No Reward

I am of the school of thought that there are no coincidences in life. I believe that absolutely everything that happens in life happens for a reason. This, therefore, makes it important that you grab opportunities each time you come across them. While some opportunities come well packaged and are very undeniable, some do not look like what you need. However, they start looking real and important when you begin to unravel them. Now, the truth remains that certain things that are considered opportunities might turn out very differently when unraveled. That notwithstanding, if you give it a try, you will almost have no regret. However, if you fail to check out an opportunity, even if you fail to admit it, you will always be full of regrets concerning how things would have turned out if only you took advantage of an opportunity. You never can tell. Sometimes, throwing caution to the wind is what you need to alter your future positively. While it is always advised that you learn to walk before you run or even fly, you should not take baby steps for too long. There are times when you should take leaps. Now, I am not saying you will always find it easy when you leap. There are, however, times when you must go all out to ensure that your status changes.

When there is life, they say there is hope. Well, if you fail to take risks, you might never get past the stage of hope. While you are alive, you can always take risks. They might not turn out as planned—that's what makes them risks in the first place.

Sometimes, taking it easy is considered a sign of intelligence. As much as this is arguable, taking it easy is also a sign of fear and the absence of courage. If you think you have a lot of fears, now is the time to know that you are not the only one with fears. Everyone has fears. However, what differentiates those that face their fears and those that don't is the ability to take risks.

In the history of the world, there at quite a few people that refuse to take the easy way out. These set of people gave up instant gratification for a long-lasting solution. One of such people is Nelson Mandela.

Nelson Mandela spent 27 years of his time on Earth in prison. He was a freedom fighter that openly opposed apartheid in South Africa. Although he was given the opportunity to walk out of prison and stop any form of demonstration, he chose to remain in prison. Today, the entire black community of South Africa is free from Apartheid because of the actions of Nelson Mandela.

Why Taking Risks Comes with Great Rewards

How To

Dreams are amazing. However, they are not known to come on a platter of gold. If you are very much interested in achieving your dreams—and at the right time, too—there are certain things that you must do. One of the most important is taking risks. It is not just enough to take risks. These risks should be properly calculated and should be worth every step. Regardless of how important it is to take chances and go through risks in life, there are lots of people that are still very scared of taking the first step.

The reward for risk might be promising. Nevertheless, it is called a risk because there is a huge likelihood that you will part with something if your plan does not fall through. When risks are involved, anything can be lost. In a business setting, when you take a risk, the most likely thing to be lost if your plans do not follow through is money. However, beyond the loss of money, there are other things of value that can be lost. Popular among them is your reputation and your time. Well, amazingly, these very things (time, reputation, and money) are some of the things that you will gain when you take calculated risks. The many gains that are associated with calculated risks can completely transform your life and business.

There are countless benefits associated with taking risks. Some are indeed obvious and stare us in the face; while others are quite hidden and must be discovered.

Jeremy Napier

When you make taking calculated risks a part of your routine, in no time you will become open to both opportunities and challenges. When done regularly, the barriers in your mind soon wear away, and you discover that you now have new mental limits along with a much-improved mental capacity.

Not many people know one way to build creativity is by taking risks. When you place yourself on the spot, your creative juices tend to flow much better than you can even imagine. This takes place because, in the absence of any excuses, it gets easy to try out something new.

It is a good thing to have a big picture of what you want. There is no rule against seeing the end of your plan right from the beginning of it. Nonetheless, not everything can be perfectly planned. You should leave some space for spontaneity. Spontaneity does not just offer you a well-deserved result when it works out; it also helps you have some fun while going through a major challenge. It is crucial to note that the chance of pulling something off when trying it for the first time is not always one hundred percent. Nonetheless, the chances are higher when you give it nothing but your best shot.

Despite what many people think, risks are not taken in the absence of logic. That is why they are better described as calculated risks. In the face of risks, it becomes much easier to come up with a definition of what it is that you want. Risks are not just taken; they are accompanied by some serious considerations. Also, taking a risk makes you want to ensure that things work out. In the absence of risks, individuals might not be sure if what they are going for is exactly what they want. However, in the presence of risks, there is always some sort of assurance that what you are going for is something that you really want.

One thing that taking risks does for you helps you break free from mediocrity and the attitude of playing safe. Risk takers never try to stay safe. They are known for forging ahead continuously in business and their chosen career paths. Risks do not just help you accomplish things; they also go a long way in building your confidence.

One thing is noteworthy: there are no guarantees in life. Sometimes, all you must do is trust your instincts and take that risk. It might not pan out well; however, you can try out the same thing several times and finally get a result.

How to Engage in Risks

Life is about taking risks. Everyone has taken risks at some point in their lives. The first risk most people take is learning to walk as a baby. When a baby learns to walk, there is no guarantee that the baby will not fall. Regardless, the baby still attempts walking. Children, in general, are not new to the idea of taking risks. Well, surprisingly, this ability to take risks reduces with age. The fact that babies must engage in risks before they can make their first step means humans were designed to take risks. Now a question arises: how can one engage in risks?

There are numerous ways to take risks. Regardless of the type of risk taken, one thing must be done first: you must evaluate the risks. Evaluating a risk properly is the only way to take a calculated risk. A lot of people fear taking risks because when risks are taken, it means they are not fully in charge of what the outcome of a situation will be. Now, taking risks does not necessarily mean going all out to get something done without first giving it thought. It simply means thinking something through intelligently and deciding that it is worth trying out. With the right amount of confidence in your abilities, taking risks and recovering from risks can be done easily.

To take a calculated risk, put down all the possible outcomes that can result from taking that risk. This should include positive outcomes, as well as negative outcomes. While at this, always bear in mind that a lot of the possibilities are associated with the risk you are about to take will not see the light of day. You should try to come up with a solution in case any of the negative possibilities that are associated with the risk you are about to take.

When trying to decide between two options (i.e., choosing between two jobs), you can't see the future. To take a calculated risk and make the right choice, consider the pros and cons of the two jobs. Once done, you should pick the job which has more pros than cons. As much

How To

as there is no guarantee that you made the right choice, the job with more pros is most likely the better one for you. This does not necessarily mean it will be right for someone else.

If you are unable to overcome the fear of disappointment, you will never be able to take a risk. The fear of disappointment can be said to be an ingredient for a life full of regrets.

If you work in a department in a firm and are not comfortable with the department you work in, you can ask for a change. Now, if you ask for a change, you cannot tell what response you will get. You might get a "yes"; or you might also get a "no." Well, if you get a "yes," that will be nice. However, if you get a "no," it will be a disappointment. That, however, will not change who you are. With a "no", you might even get an idea of how well you have been performing on your job.

Risks are never comfortable. When you are out of your comfort zone, you become more comfortable when faced with an uncertain situation. Now, the inability to tell what the outcome of an event will be can make one anxious. Regardless of this, the longer you are out of your comfort zone, the less anxious you will be in the middle of uncertainty.

A simple way of starting with this is to write down a list of uncertainties in your life. Ensure you write them down from the most anxious to the least anxious. Now, when you have them written down, begin to face these situations on purpose from the least uncertain to the most uncertain.

Jeremy Napier

Basic Facts You Need to Know About Taking Risks

The path of which is associated with risks is a path that a lot of people fear taking. The reason for this is it is a path that not many people have gone through. This means it does not have a clearly defined track for people to walk through. The implication of this is the easiest way to get through this part successfully is to rely on your instincts. Unfortunately, our instincts are not always right and can make us do the wrong things sometimes. Amazingly, the opportunities which are usually on roads that have not been traveled by many people are usually untapped. As a result of this, the few people that are ready to take the risk to go through this path are usually highly rewarded.

Often, the disappointments we face when we take risks do not have much to do with us. If they have anything to do with us at all, it is usually just a little. Most disappointments we experience when we take risks are associated with other factors aside from us. As a result of this, when we take calculated risks, there is little to nothing we can do to alter the outcome. Not taking a risk is as good as being disappointed because of a risk taken. The reason for this is with risks, disappointments are usually instantaneous. However, in the absence of risks, disappointments still occur. This time, they occur after a long time and might not give you any chance to recover.

In as much as the best way to get the best out of a situation is to be always prepared for such a situation. There are times when we must make moves even if we are not prepared. Although preparing ahead of time is believed will help anyone get the best out of a situation, this is not always the case. In some situations, disappointments still occur even after adequate preparations. In this same way, one can get the best out of a situation by just following their instincts and not having any real form of preparation.

Risks will not always turn out positive. When we take risks and succeed, it is a good thing. However, when we take risks and fail, we only fail when we give up. If we don't give up, we will figure out a different way to get things to work; it will just take a little more time.

When you take a risk, there is no guarantee that things will pan out as planned. This is more reason you should take risks earlier in life. If you take a risk early and things go south, you will always have time to get back on your feet. However, if you take a risk quite late, you really might never get back on your feet if things go bad.

Chapter 7:
Judging A Book by Its Cover Will Be Your Downfall

The average person knows that judging others is not exactly a good thing. Why do I know this? Well, nobody wants to be judged; everyone wants to be understood. To a large extent, we are all guilty of judging others. While at this, however, only very few of us realize that judging others can lead to our downfall.

Imagine you come across a seemingly harmless beggar on the street, and you think such a person is too healthy to be begging anyway. You get close to this beggar, and they take out a gun and point at you. You are surprised and must flee. Well, a few days later, the news gets to you that the beggars around the place you met a beggar are usually victims of kidnappers. Suddenly, your perception of this beggar will change. You formerly judged them for begging because you thought they could do better. You were even more surprised when the beggar pulled a gun. Well, with the knowledge that beggars are usually victims of kidnappers, you understand the situation better, and it all makes perfect sense to you. This is not a real-life situation. It does, however, gives you an idea of what judging people is like.

How To

You see, ideally when you come across someone that you feel is too good to be begging, instead of being judgmental, you should have questions on your mind. These questions can be "why are they begging? What can you do to help?" In as much as being judgmental is more of an instinct than asking questions regarding why people are in certain situations, it is important to train yourself to exhaust all alternatives before speaking.

So, with a mindset that is more compassionate and less judgmental, when you see someone that you consider too good to be begging, you can see the situation differently. As soon as you see this individual, you are curious and do not judge. You begin to wonder why they are begging in the first place and what can be done to help them. Now, even if you fail in helping them, you will not give them a proud look.

As a person, it is expedient that you learn to look beyond people's backgrounds and their present states. Seeing the potential in people is good quality. Give people opportunities instead of judging them.

Why Do People Judge Others?

Although a lot of us might not admit this fact, somewhere in our subconscious, we think that individuals with the same physical appearance have the same type of behavior. This is perhaps why it is easy to hate an individual that looks like someone that hurt you in the past.

Now, people associating certain behavior to a certain physical appearance might be common when looks are involved. Nonetheless, it does not end at that. Peoples speech pattern, their way of walking, and even the way they dress can make it easy to associate them with a certain type of behavior. If while growing up, someone that was repeatedly nice to you was known for wearing a shape of prescriptive lenses, there is a tendency that you will be very comfortable with people that wear that shape of prescriptive lenses. This is irrespective of what you have heard about them.

When you come across a person, the first thing you probably notice is such a person's body language and physical appearance. Irrespective of the fact that that is not all we see; a lot of people do not realize this.

As individuals, sometimes we forget some things. However, when we come across people that remind us of some of these experiences, the memories come rushing back. If you had a negative experience with someone and you meet another person that has some striking similarities with the person that hurt you, it is just natural that you will dislike this new person. Now, if this person does something that is slightly hurtful, you are most likely going to overreact because you will be associating their action with that of someone that you already dislike.

In as much as the reason above, if one of the generally accepted reasons why people judge others, it is not the only reason. Sometimes, we judge people because they have certain characteristics which we really will never accept from ourselves. A simple example is this: When a shy person meets an outgoing person, even if that outgoing person is not a show-off, it is almost natural for the shy person to judge them as being too loud. Generally, shy people will never be the center of attention. As a result of this, when another person is always the center of attention, they might consider that person a show-off.

Judging Others Is Bad for You

Not everyone knows this, but judging other people is bad for them. It ruins their reputation without even giving them a chance to prove themselves. Well, judging others is not only bad for them, but it is also bad for you. You might not realize this, but there are lots of negative effects of judging others on the individual carrying out judgment.

It is amazing how there are good judgments and bad judgments. Still, most people dwell on just bad judgments. Often, bad judgments are carried out on people's physical appearances, religion, social status, skin color, and dressing.

Always judging others is a habit; just like other bad habits, it can be stopped. When you judge others, you are doing yourself so much harm. You know why? You are stopping your mind from seeing both sides of a person. When done constantly, it makes you myopic, and you end up having a closed mind. Now, being close-minded is almost as bad as being uneducated.

Jeremy Napier

If you judge others before getting to know them, you should know one thing for sure: the problem is not with them, the problem is with you.

A lot of people are of the idea that judging others ends with just strangers or people that you do not know well. Well, contrary to that thought, when judging others becomes a habit for you, it is only a matter of time before you start judging individuals that are very close to you. This soon degenerates to a lack of appreciations and ultimately dissatisfaction. When you become judgmental of the people around you, it will put a strain on your relationships.

Now, if you have a strained relationship with people that are closest to you, no one will view you in a positive light. According to research, the ability of an individual to always see the best in other people says a lot about such a person's personality. Seeing the positive side of people is associated with being kind-hearted, emotionally stable, and happy. The exact opposite can be said about people that are always in the habit of judging others, especially when this judgment is negative.

When you see the positive side of other people, it is proof that you have lots of positive traits. However, when all you see is the negative side of people, you can be certain that a lot of people have negative views about you.

When you constantly judge people in front of other people, it is only normal for your audience to assume that you will judge them in front of others, too. The reason for this is quite straight forward: a lot of people will feel that if you can talk poorly to them about other people, then you can say bad things to others about them. This will make them distrust you.

People Are Not Who You Think They Are

Have you heard the saying, "don't judge a book by its cover?" Appearances are often misleading and are not always an accurate representation of who people are. Going by this, you should never judge people by their appearance. Some appear the way they do because they want to always maintain a low key. Others, because they cannot afford expensive things. Regardless of how peoples' appearances are, always consider the good they have done before concluding them.

Reasons Why You Should Not Judge Other People

There are lots of reasons—possible inexhaustible—why judging other people is bad. Most people judge individuals that they know little-to-nothing about. You see, it is important that you know people quite well before ever attempting to judge them. It is rather unfortunate that most people do the exact opposite of that.

People differ in many ways. Even siblings that have been raised in the same house differ in very striking ways. If by chance, you do not enjoy taking part in an activity, it does not necessarily mean that other people do not love that activity. Take this as an example. If you do not like to braid your hair as a guy, it does not mean other people have to hate the same thing. It is wrong for you to go on and tell people that their braided hair does not look great. If you have a university degree and some other person does not, it does not imply that they could not pass their examinations, or they do not know the value of education. It could simply mean that they could not afford to pay for a university education. You see, we differ in lots of ways. The fact that people are different from you does not mean that you are right, and they are wrong.

There are certain people that are indeed better than those around them—this fact notwithstanding, no one that is perfect. There are, however, people that believe that they are perfect. As a result of this, they go on to judge everyone around them and have a habit of always picking on other people's mistakes. Before going ahead to criticize anyone's actions, you should be certain that this criticism is constructive and not merely to bring such person down.

Judging others may come with a feeling of guilt. There are just a handful of people that do not feel guilty when they judge others. Those people are usually regarded as horrible, and I want to assume that they are not a horrible person. I am assuming they are not a horrible person because you are going through this write-up.

Now that you recognize guilt associated with judging others, it is important that you get the best out of this feeling. There is a tendency to let this feeling overwhelm you; however, what you need to do is make it a weapon to serve as an impediment to the attitude of judging others.

Searching for A Reason to Stop Judging People, Well, Here's One

If you have made judging people a habit, one of the best things you can do is to stop judging people. Well, it is one thing to want to quit judging people and another thing to know exactly how to stop judging people.

The first step for anyone that wants to stop judging people is to be aware they're judging. If you are unaware of a bad habit, how are you going to stop?

Picture this: You have a distant relative that has just gone through a very painful breakup. She is depressed and begins overeating. She does not stop at overeating; she also begins drinking. She does all this to mask the pain of the breakup. Her health starts failing, yet she does not stop the bad habits of drinking and overeating. At this point, you may judge her for the bad habits she has. You think she is responsible for her bad health.

Now, the truth remains that her habits are wrong and will not cause a change of any form. Regardless, she does not deserve to be judged. There is a huge likelihood of your awareness of the bad things she is doing to herself. However, you might be ignorant of the root cause of those habits. Well, what is taking place is your relative has just gone through a breakup and is now depressed. She tries to eat and drink to make herself feel happy and take away the pain. We all do things to make ourselves happy when we go through difficulties, even if these things are not so bad for our health.

It takes a lot of practice for you to stop judging people. It is a very bad thing to judge. Sometimes you do not have to tell others about the negative attitude of some people before you judge them. If you find yourself constantly complaining about an individual, then you are most likely judging such an individual.

Once you discover that you are judging someone, there are questions that you must ask yourself, including: "What are the reasons I am judging?" Do I have expectations that are unrealistic?" Do I know what the person am judging is going through?" What do I love about the person I am judging?" How would I act if I were in the shoes of the person I am judging?"

As soon as you are done asking yourself all these questions, ask yourself how you can be of aid to the person. Does this person have any needs? Most times, the person you are judging has some real needs. Other times, all they need is someone that will listen to them and accept them for who they are.

You see, if you must be of help to the people you judge, you can't go on judging them. You cannot only come to their aid when you keep judging them but see what they go through with eyes of empathy. The amazing part of this is that as soon as you are curious about what they are going through and are successfully able to help them, you will be a lot more fulfilled than you will ever be when judging others.

Benefits of Not Judging

When you avoid judging people, you are better focused on your goals. You see, when you put in so much effort and a lot of energy into judging others, you have less time to focus on the things that are important to you. Passing judgment on people makes you think about irrelevant things. You end up spending time on things that are not your business. These things, therefore, take the place of the thoughts you really should be having.

You achieve more when you spend less time judging the world—it's that simple. I'm sure you might say, "I'm not judgmental." Well, here is a question to munch on: have you ever made assumptions about strangers walking down the street? Yes? Such thoughts can separate you from achieving success.

It is quite normal for people to avoid environments where they believe they will be judged. This is not exactly a bad thing. However, if you tend to always judge others, this becomes a major issue. The reason for this is you will always think people will judge you and will do everything to avoid places where you will be judged. This might work for a short while. It will, however, bring about a lot of limitations. The amazing thing is some of the best leaders in the world have been constantly judged. Now, if you avoid certain environments because you think you will be judged, you will be limited by yourself greatly.

Don't ever judge a person by their background. You never really know someone or how much drive they must want to succeed. Always treat them with respect as it could open new opportunities. Measuring a person by their heart and hard work will always preserve.

Chapter 8:
You Can't Conquer the World Alone

Life is a mystery, and the decisions we make either make or mark our lifestyle. The truth is, we are different, and we have various perspectives to solving personal problems. There are no laid down rules in handling personal issues. At some point in our lives, we need a support system to face life challenges squarely—because no one can conquer the world alone.

Certain individuals become emotionally drained when hit to the rocks, while others take it as a steppingstone to run life's race. Just to be clear, we all have our strong and weak moments in life. Additionally, we are designed differently in terms of psychological behavior. But many people are feeble-minded and often are trampled by others. This in a way brings an unconscious lock up because they fear what would become of them when they speak about their phobias and secrets. But you know the truth? It is safer talking to someone about a challenge, especially when it is of a great burden. Also, when the mess is so deep, we need a hand to pull us out from it. Managing emotional stress, breakups, health issues, and depression can be mind-tricky often. We all at some time have fallen victim of this situation. We have unconsciously shut ourselves out from the rest of the world when it was too much to bear.

I, for one, do not dispute the fact that there are situations that warrant personal decisions or lone thoughts. Also, you would agree with me that there are emotional predicaments which require external help from relatives and friends. So, we need to strike a balance to make sure none outweighs the other. When life challenges pop up, building unseen walls or shutting others out should be the least imagination to envisage; this would only be harmful to you. And for this reason, making the right connection in terms of friendships and relationships would be a call of victory to one's emotional and mental metamorphosis.

Choosing the Right Friends

Although some individuals are naturally introverted because they focus primarily on their feelings, it is no reason to have restricted association with others. Studies have shown that humans have a ground-laying need to be associated with others, and "association" can be referred to as "friendship." Just as food is a necessity for human survival, so is friendship.

We perform best when our hunger is quenched, and this is a natural-born instinct because we are social animals. When our social chords are cut off, we become emotionally and physically traumatized. Being without friends poses a danger known as depression. And this intellectual consciousness replays through our brain, leading to an emotional breakdown. Therefore, to face the varied challenges of life, we need to stay motivated with friends.

What is Friendship?
Friendship may be described as a type of relationship distinguished by a feeling of care, affection, and concern between two people. Interestingly, it would surprise you that some friends, in the long run, turn into families. They support us in our down times and put a smile on our face. So, choosing a friend is not something you do hurriedly; it is brain tasking, and of course, it takes time and wisdom to build such a relationship. Although, there are moments when you meet a person, and it feels like you've known them a lifetime; this should not in any way be misinterpreted because not everyone is worth being friends with. Even times when friends become lovers, their attitude changes; a certain number of individuals feel more comfortable with the transition, while others regret the transition. So, maximum caution needs to be taken while choosing the right friend to lean on. An example would be portrayed again in this chapter for a better understanding.

More Than Just Friends
Kimberly and Josh started off as friend's freshman year, and as time passed, the chemistry between them surfaced and grew. They became best friends after a while and had a relationship one would refer to as perfect; of a truth, it was. They were so in love and wanted

the whole world to know about it. They connected and understood each other in ways another other couples' thought was impossible. Most of the time, they were seen hanging out together even though they majored in different courses; it was a moment of true friendship for them, and they enjoyed every bit of it. But as semesters swiftly passed, things changed. Everyone thought the two best friends were inseparable. However, they were on the brink of losing their trust and respect for each other. Josh, on his own end, became emotionally attached to someone else while Kimberly thought of ways to salvage the lost hope in their relationship. Oops! Life happens, and it was no one's fault; after all, emotions cannot be totally controlled since it's a raging force on its own.

The sudden change in Josh's new affection shattered her heart, and she became emotionally miserable. He became demanding, selfish, and used every opportunity to demean her before their colleagues and friends. No doubt, he became toxic and suffocating to her. Bit by bit, Kimberly lost her self-confidence until she was engulfed with insecurity and consequently depression.

Alas, she had made Josh her emotional anchor, and now she feels adrift. She literally cried herself to sleep every night and without thorough thought, decided to also be in a new relationship. However, she sought a relationship in her moment of weakness. Yes, she found the wrong set of people, who made her sink deeper into her shell.

How To

Gradually, she found herself abusing drugs and before she knew it, she became addicted.

You can imagine the additional heartache and devastation. The only crime she ever committed was to find love again, but instead, life welcomed her into her cold embrace of filth and disgust. For a long while, the feeling and experience could not be erased from her mind because of the toxicity it had implanted in her. And this, I would say, made her a shadow of herself. She inherently crawled up into a shell and shut the rest of the world out.

So, I would like to ask you, what do you think changed in their relationship?

I'm very certain if Kimberly was given a plain sheet to start all over, she would erase ever meeting Josh. But unluckily, this has become a story she would tell all through her lifetime. Most times, we have no control over emotions, our future, or the people we meet. But most, we have a choice to accept or decline what we want in our lives.

Some relationships have a way of jeopardizing our friendship and can be termed toxic because it affects our mental health. A toxic relationship can be described as a time bomb; it continuously ticks until it someday explodes. It never gets better no matter the effort you put in. Need I say more? A killjoy is what it is. One of the many things it does is confiscate your peace of mind daily. So, I ask, why be in a toxic relationship when you can achieve much more?

Well, we might not make the right choices at the first instance; since everyone puts on their best behavior mode. We are mostly blinded by our emotions and then become victims of the negative outcome of relationships. You have a right to decide what you'd make out of a messed-up life. Different individual's pass-through similar or worse situations than this every day. But the top-notch secrets that have kept them moving with the train of life is their ability to persevere and their capacity to pick up the broken pieces of whatever life was shattered.

Dangers of Loneliness

In line with many experts, loneliness and "being alone" have been interchangeably used to mean the same; but there is a clear distinction between the two words. Loneliness can be a result of several things, but that is not the case with "being alone." For some persons, having a self-timer or being alone can be a choice. As a matter of fact, during my teen years, there were moments I stayed alone. It was not depression or suicidal thoughts taking hold on me; I wanted to be "alone."

Some research has shown that loneliness and unhealthy relationships substantially damage the physical and emotional well-being of a person. And, if not detected and dealt with in time, can pose a great risk to their immune system and mental health. Also, it can lead to several medical complications such as depression, anxiety, and high-level stress; actually, it is a silent health killer. Anyways, it is of great essence to know that no one consciously chooses to be in this state of mind; it gradually creeps in because it is a feeling on its own. More so, because we have no control over it, it gradually turns us into its puppet. Also, death is another factor that contributes to loneliness. This sad feeling can cause psychological trauma for some individuals; especially when the person happens to be a spouse to the deceased. We have various ways of grieving, yes, but others grief more and so suffers setbacks like loneliness.

Deciding

Often, we tend to live in a secluded box we create. And this, I would say, is the greatest harm anyone can cause to themselves emotionally. The choice to speak, to make new friends, to leave for a new location, to try a different relationship, or even a skill can be the best decision to make in a lifetime. Decision making comes along with sacrifices, and surprisingly, not everyone can make sacrifices. So, the big question is: are you ready to make any sacrifice for your happiness? They say talk is cheap, but actions speak louder than voice. Most, there are a quite number of things that need to be taken off the shelf while making life decisions. Also, there are a lot of other things that we need to embrace while coming out of a shell. As unbelievable as they may sound, they have been proven to help individuals overcome toxic relationships and loneliness:

The Gradual Breakthrough

As much as we want to be left with our thoughts, we also need to learn to "let go" of our toxic past. I mean past that would hinder our emotional breakthrough. Do you see it? There are no perfect lives or relationships anywhere. Happy endings only exist in movies and novels. They are nothing but fiction; they never happen in the actual world. In the real world, everyone battles with one hidden character or the other, and it's been since time's past. If you also care to know, we have no Prince Charming or Miss Snow White in this real world. We are all the same evolving individuals trying to salvage our lifestyle to a certain acceptable percentage.

Have A Mentor

Before going into details about what mentorship is, it is necessary to know that not all persons have mentors; this decision does not in any way make them unserious with life pursuit, nor does it mean failure for them; they just do not see it as a necessity or a trophy to be won. These individuals perform better without mentors. In contrary, persons suffering from loneliness or emotional trauma need a lot of mentoring to gradually rehabilitate. What then is mentorship? Mentorship is a type of relationship in which a more knowledgeable person in a carved niche helps a less experienced person. For instance, if I am going through a phase and at the same time feeling depressed, getting a mentor or a person to lean on would help revive my lost hope.

Finally, asking for the big help!

How To

It is one thing to be around friends, mentors, and relatives. Also, it is a different ball game to be able to confide in them. Emotional help does not come cheap; actually, it takes a long time to entrust your thoughts to someone else. But first things first: learn to seek help from those around; before you learn the hard way. Furthermore, you need to "accept the truth of the past." This is the key to emotional freedom. To put it in a more pronounced way, I would prefer we said, "making peace with the past."

There are wars we can never win, and there are situations we may never "undo." But it takes real courage to accept the losses and wins of life. Oh, did I forget to say Kimberly overcame her traumas? Yeah, she did surprisingly. It was tough, and it was not an easy sail, but she did anyway; because she asked for help. I want you to know that no one will run around offering you a helping hand—you ask for it. Remember, the mind is not a transparent glass. So, until you ask for help, no one would give it to you freely. Then what must you do? Ask, talk, and keep talking until you find that which would liberate you from the toxic emotion.

In addition to making peace with the past, one needs to "admit their fault."

Truthfully it can be a hard task to do because no one wants to take the blame for their wrongdoings. We think it is safer playing the victim to get more sympathy; that feeling can be overwhelming, yes, but that will only cause more harm than good. Recognizing one's fault in a failed relationship is not an easy decision to make. But it is a big step to freedom. We are imperfect, and we are humans and as such are bound to make mistakes.

Freedom

The word freedom has a wide range of meaning. For an inmate, freedom means to be released from prison. For a democratic country, it means an unconstrained way of talking or behaving as citizens. Nonetheless, for some it might be termed as "a light at the end of a tunnel." This five-letter word "light" has liberated many from seen and unseen dark moments. Just as breakups starts from the mind before it becomes a physical detachment, freedom also comes from ones thought.

To break free might seem impossible at the first but try and never stop. Scream and cry if there is a need to, but don't stop trying because negative emotional encapsulation can be deadly. Truthfully, humans can be selfish. But also, no one wants to have a feeling of guilt for not helping. So, my candid advice to you: seek help to gain your emotional freedom, because you cannot conquer the world alone.

Chapter 9:
The Power of Your Mind is Limitless

You are blessed with the most advanced and complex machinery that has ever existed—your mind. Man, out of all the living things on Earth, has an edge that goes beyond evolution: he has the power to create the world he desires. Just think it, and it will happen that house you've always envisioned for you and your family; that exotic vacation destination, a rich bank account. It's that simple. Even though we come across materials that tell us about the unlimited power of the mind, we have yet to grasp the true meaning of it. Perhaps, we may never get to truly understand how vast our minds are.

From the moment we are born, we are granted the ability to interact with our environment, and to form thoughts and perception based on our experiences. It is during these formative years that we learn from our parents, teachers, peers, and community. Sometimes, those who surround us unconsciously pass on and stamp their perception and beliefs about life. More so, we tend to create our perceptions based on these. Unfortunately, we create an unending circle of limitations.

Consequently, we feel powerless and live our lives on autopilot without a thought of breaking the self-inflicted barriers we've placed in our minds. Despite our extraordinary minds, we are depressed, disconnected, mentally unfit, and apathetic. Some can break free from these limitations and finally get to harness their potentials. These people are the ones you see as being blessed with everything you've ever desired for yourself. So, what sets you apart from those who seem to have it all?

Your Conscious Thoughts Set the Ball Rolling

Your answer lies in your conscious thought. Yes, your conscious thought is responsible for every decision you make, and this reflects in your subconscious which dictates your outcome. For instance, if you tell yourself, "I will win and be the best," you are conditioning your subconscious thoughts to align your outcome to that declaration. Therefore, if we don't have conscious control over our conscious thoughts, our lives will become like a ship without a rudder. Changing your conscious thought is a sure-fire to unlocking the vast potentials of your mind. Before we delve into how you can unlock your mind power, I'll like to explore the dangers of our reality.

Ironically, Reality Is A Blindfold

Let's be realistic; man cannot create machines for flying. Let's be realistic; it's impossible for a human to run 1000 miles in 11 days. Let's be realistic; there's no way a virtual currency can work. Yes, these are the words we hear every day. Perhaps, we say it quite a lot. Let's be realistic; I can't have that dream car with my salary. It's so easy to fall into the trap of reality. We mostly use it as a shield to protect us from experiencing hurt or disappointment. Over time, we've made it our defense mechanism. Unconsciously, these words have the power to limit your thinking power. No matter, how much you earn or try out different activities, you will never pass the limit of reality. Here's a question for you: have you ever seen any successful person utter those words? I'm sure the answer is no. Why? For you to break barriers and unlock your mind, you need to ignore the laws of reality. Reality will tell you that those who are born in a certain country or condition are prone to certain factors. More so, reality often works in conduction with research and statistics, to keep you under check.

People often see reality as their only truth. Well, this approach is wrong, as most people often associate reality with limitations and failure. I'm not disputing the fact that reality helps us to get in-tune with society. However, you should learn how to peer behind the curtains of reality, especially when it blocks your goals. Mind you, the only way you can accomplish that is to learn the art of positive thinking. Yes, positive thinking is a term we've come across in different motivational speeches and books. This concept is what you need to unlock the limitations of your mind. You might ask, "Why is it so important?" Not to worry, as we will explore this concept in the next section.

Positivity Is the Key to Unlocking Your Mind Power

Jeremy Napier

I admit, maintaining a positive outlook is difficult for some, while it comes easily to others; it's a continuous struggle for some people due to constant life-changing circumstances. Therefore, you need to learn the art of positive thinking and how to integrate it into your conscious thought. By doing this, it will become a habit, hence impacting other aspects of your life. As mentioned earlier, positive thinking is a skill, and there are four stages you need to pass through before it becomes a habit. Personally, these stages have helped me to integrate and live positively even when faced with fierce challenges.

Hold on! You need to know that these stages that might not work for everyone who wants to learn positive thinking

You don't know how much power you have over your thoughts. This is a common problem with so many people: they find it difficult to see the world through another perspective. Their life experience has made them rigid; hence, pessimistic and unwilling to have a paradigm shift. When you realize that it is possible for you to learn positivity via a paradigm shift, then you are on the first step toward success. Acknowledge this fact, and let's move on to the next stage.

Positive thinking can be learned. More so, it can be cultivated until it becomes all you know. It's not enough to learn positive thinking; you need to know how to put it in action. No doubt, this is the hardest and perhaps the most exhausting stage. Why? Because it involves acting. Study people with a positive outlook on life, read books and materials on positive thinking. Never stop even when it's hard: your results are closer than you think.

When you reach this last stage, you have finally unlocked the power of positive thinking. This is the time when the act of thinking positively comes naturally, even when you don't feel positive. Although you might not feel positive all the time, your thoughts will always look for the good or silver lining in any situation. Just as the adage says, "you never forget how to ride a bike," if you practice more at positive thinking, it will become more of a habit.

To make positive thinking a habit, here a few ways you need to practice.

Start with Affirmations
Otherwise known as positive statements, these words have much more impact on your lives than you could ever imagine. Let's try out some positive affirmations:

"I am so grateful and happy for (fill in the blank space with whatever you are thankful for)."

Mind you, it doesn't matter how insignificant it seems. Here's another for you to try:

"It's so wonderful to (fill it with whatever you wish)."

Tell me how does it feel saying those affirmations aloud? More confident? Assured of a better tomorrow? Now imagine repeating it continuously until it becomes a habit. The truth is, most people unconsciously make negative affirmations about themselves or their circumstances in life. Gradually, we find ourselves going down the path of these negative statements. To avoid negative outcomes, we need to consciously make positive statements that works with positive emotions, such as being happy and grateful. Remember, it's more than saying these words; you must try and feel the emotion of the words.

Discard Pessimism and Embrace Optimism

Earlier, I explained the dangers of being realistic when optimism is needed. You need to have an optimistic view about life irrespective of your past or present circumstances. Ask yourself about the outcome you want. The outcome could relate to a goal in your life. Start by thinking of a positive income and expect the best no matter what.

Walk with The Right People

It is never too much to mention that you need to walk with the right set of people. I'm talking about those with a goal-getting mindset. According to philosopher John Rohm, "we are an average of those we spend the most time with." Here's something you might not have noticed: those you spend your time with have an impact on your emotions and thoughts. If you suddenly feel depressed, look at those who are by your side. There's a high chance your mood was triggered by something they said or did.

Be Grateful
Why should I be grateful when things don't play out the way I want? Well, you should know that there are many people who would give an arm and leg to be in your situation. Think you have it rough? Wait until you walk in another's shoes. Gratitude will help you to keep your mind on the positive, so you don't have time to think of the negatives in your life. It is not enough to say the words of gratitude; you must feel nervous before them. Confused on how to go about it? Here's a trick that has worked for me. Keep a gratitude journal. Try writing at least five things you feel grateful for and see how your attitude toward life changes.

Substitute "Have" With "Get"
Still having trouble with adopting a positive habit. Try substituting the word "have" with "get." Do you observe how many times we say we "have:" to do something? It happens all the time. I must write. I must complete this project. I must go to work. I must prepare the kids for school. Now change the word "have" to "get." I get to complete this project. I get to write; I get to go to work. Even, I get to pay my rent. What do you notice with this little change? Your attitude changes immediately from needing to fulfill obligations to being grateful for the things we've become accustomed to having: a roof over your head,

kids, a job, a talent. Once you make this change, you will become happier, and it will unlock the limits you've placed on your mind.

Avoid Emotional Deadweight

Let's say your day was going well, but then you go to school or work and your colleague starts complaining about his life, job, or family. You didn't think about it before he/she brought it up. However, you find yourself agreeing and joining the bandwagon of complainants. Don't fall into the trap. According to research, complaining leads to depression, emotional and motivational deficits.

Take A Deep Breath

One of the reasons why yoga is so popular is because it offers us an outlet for our stress, frustrations, and negative emotions. What's more interesting is that breathing exercises are a core component of yoga practices. Your breathing is connected to your emotions. For instance, your breathing becomes fast and irregular if you have a panic attack. More so, your breath slows down when you are expecting or concentrating on something. Since you now understand the link between your breath and emotions, you can work toward controlling it.

Hold on To the Success Stories

Daily we hear stories of people losing their humanity, hunger, war, and natural disasters. It's difficult to have hope and stay positive when we hear such stories. However, we rarely see stories of people who rise during these trying times to make stronger change. Well, it's time to watch out for those success stories. Look out for the person who saved so many people during a natural disaster. Look out for those who fight against injustice, and there lies your beacon of positivity.

Make Others Smile

We mostly think of ourselves—yes, it's alright to take responsibility for ourselves. But set a target to make someone smile in a day. This time around, look outward instead of inward. Think about others' happiness, and this will help you to realize the impact of your attitude and expression on others.

Chapter 10:
Awaking the Giant when Defeated and Broken

We carry immense power within us. A power so great, it dwarfs our wildest imagination—it's limitless. We all have it. It's what makes us special in our way. The janitor at your office or school has it. Each of us has a unique power; your CEO has this immense power, even your colleagues have it. Now, here's a question: if we truly possess this immense power or giant within us, why are we in our current position? Why do we feel dejected and incapable if we have this immense power at our disposal?

Furthermore, if we have the same power as the elites, why are we not up there? Doesn't seem to add up, right? The answer is simple: we've simply lost sight of who we are. We have buried the giant within us underneath heaps and loads of worries, low self-esteem, our lackadaisical attitude, and in discipline. Our present condition has become our sole reality. Yes, we forget that we are so much more while we look on with envy at those who have awakened that power within them. Well, my dear reader, it's time. I know you are ready. The fact that you read this book to this stage means you are ready to cast off your old self and kickstart the process to awaken your power. In this chapter, you will not only learn how to awaken the giant within you, but how you create a compelling future for yourself and your loved ones. However, you need first to clear away the rubble that has buried your giant. Yes, you need first to learn how to believe in yourself.

Believe in Yourself

While growing up, some of our dreams were squashed by those who thought they were looking out for us. For instance, a child who shows an interest in drawing would be told about the financial hardship which befalls most artists. They take it a step further by saying that the child wouldn't achieve anything if he or she continues that path. Little by little, this unhealthy advice begins to chip away at the child's self-confidence in that skill and gradually spreads into other aspects of the child's life. Sadly, the voice never leaves even when we become adults and have families of our own. The voice taunts you when you summon the courage to start a goal. More so, it criticizes you when things get difficult and use it as proof of your incompetence. Yes, it's not easy to contain self-doubt since it sneaks up on you when you are unaware. Self-doubt is greedy and when let loose, devours our confidence and strips reason and logic from your mind. More so, it leaves you with fear and insecurity. Sometimes, you try to remove self-doubt with positive thinking, but it's not as effective as you might want. Here's what you've been doing wrong: self-doubt is not a depressing beast. Rather, it's a part of human nature, just like joy and happiness. You need to embrace self-doubt to believe in yourself. If you want to believe in yourself, you need to first identify your self-doubts. You can identify self-doubt when you utter sentences like, "I can't, "What if? "and "I have to..." Do away with such negative sentences and practice the following steps to believe in yourself.

Believe It's Possible

You will always have the nay-sayers around you: those who will tell you it's impossible. Don't listen to them. Rather, take hold of your mind and steer it to deliver the outcome you want. You just must discipline your mind to believe in possible expectations, and events will line up to give you that desired outcome.

Visualize Your Destination

Envision what your life would look like if you achieved your dreams. Remember, the mind is a powerful tool and motivator. By visualizing your destination, it will give you the needed to boost to reach your goal. You will notice you are unexpectedly doing tasks that move you closer to your dreams. You will find yourself volunteering to take on more responsibility, asking directly for what you want, taking the lead at board meetings, and eating healthy. Here's an effective way to carry out this step: I want you to create a visualization board. This is a graphic representation of your goals, and you can always go back to it when you feel less motivated.

Act as If You've Arrived at Your Destination

How To

Let's say you dream of becoming a millionaire in the next few years. Ask yourself, "what type of friends would I keep when I become a millionaire? What about the clothes you would wear at that stage? Would you give a certain portion of your investment to charities or religious places?" One of the best and effective ways of establishing a successful mindset is to behave as if you are already the type of person who has achieved their goals. Whatever actions you identify, start doing them now.

Let's say you want to become a supermodel in the next five years. Start eating the type of strict diet you would eat when you finally become a supermodel. By doing this, you can condition your subconscious mind to find creative ways to achieve your goals.

Become the Best You Can Be

Once you are free from the depressing rubble of self-doubt, it's time to awaken that latent power within you. It's time to become the premium version of who you are. I want you to take into consideration that we have different perception about the best version of ourselves. Despite the difference in perception, one thing is common: your happiest version is the best version of yourself. Yes, happiness plays a huge part in this journey. No doubt, it is common to see many people belittle the significance of achieving their goals. I've seen so many people downplay the immense importance of happiness in attaining their goals. So, let's look at how to create your happiness since your best version is majorly dependent on it.

Jeremy Napier

Creating Your Own Happiness

Who's in charge of your happiness? The answer is you. The choice to be happy or unhappy is the easiest thing in the world to accomplish. All you must do is decide. Have you ever wondered why children are the happiest? Their happiness stems from their inability to get weighed down by the circumstances of adulthood. If you ask a child what makes him/her happy, I'm sure they would talk about things we regard as mundane. For instance, they would talk about a fast train rushing by, streets lights shining on a river, a swallow flying, birds in the sky, and so much more. The kids can see the essence and wives/wonders of the world we live in. No doubt, to become happy you need to see through the eyes of children—without judgment. Happiness is achievable, but most people consciously and unconsciously manufacture their unhappiness. Although some unhappiness is caused by social conditions, these are of lesser proportion to that which we create by ourselves. Yes, most of our unhappiness comes from within, and it's time to let it go. You need to learn how to create your happiness to be the best version of yourself.

Our happiness majorly stems from cultivating the habit of the mind. In other words, cultivate the happiness habit, and your life will become a continuous feast. You can cultivate the happiness habit through positive thinking. It's quite straightforward, as we have discussed in the previous chapter. Create a mental list of happy thoughts and replay it in your mind every day. It's normally for a stray, unhappy thought to creep into your mind occasionally. When it does, substitute it with a happy thought.

Here's a lay-your-bed principle for happiness: every morning before rising, run a few happy thoughts through your mind. These happy thoughts will create a ripple effect that affects other habits and tasks for the day.

Know Who You Want to Be

Firstly, know the type of person you aspire to become. Create a list of the important qualities in your personality. Slow and regain your composure if you find yourself deviating from these important qualities. For instance, you want to become a happy person, come up with a plan to practice happiness even in stressful conditions.

Secondly, set achievable goals. Don't fall into the quagmire of setting unrealistic goals that will leave you frustrated and spent at the end. So, set specific and achievable goals which are easy to fulfill. In addition to this, you will feel good about them.

Thirdly, prepare for success. Always try to be one step ahead and eliminate things that might impede your progress. No doubt, being prepared will help you to feel less overwhelmed and stressed. At this point, do away with procrastination. Prepare for the next day's or week's tasks.

Lastly, surround yourself with energy boosters. Your energy boosters are those who support you and cheer you on with positive words. Don't spend time with toxic people. Furthermore, be a source of motivation and positive words to people.

Make Lifestyle Changes

Start by getting rid of the "junks" in your schedule, home, and life. It's just important to cut away the unnecessary parts of your life, to have an increased benefit in your specified area. If you have too much stuff or commitment, get rid of it. Since unnecessary things can cloud up your judgment, declutter your home, streamline your finances, and cut away unnecessary commitments.

Learn to say "no." We sometimes bite more than we can chew. It's alright to refuse some projects if you don't have the time to handle. Remember, it's better to say no than to perform below par on a project. Only include things you want to do in your priority list. More so, you can delegate tasks to others if your schedule is filled up.

Perform Self-Assessment. It's alright to gauge yourselves to see if you are still on the path of success or not through your thoughts and habits. Hold on! Don't judge yourself too harshly during self-assessment. Furthermore, create a plan to reduce your failures in the future.

Create a Plan to Achieve Your Goals. Most people don't think of the plan through which they will attain their goals. Start by dividing your goals into long-term or short-term. Create deadlines for these goals and formulate a plan to attain them. To help you fare better, use a daily planner to help allocate the time you need for each goal.

Invest in Yourself

It starts with you: everything you achieve starts with you. Therefore, it's only right to take care of yourself mentally and physically to achieve what you desire. Eat well, exercise regularly, get enough rest, and address your health issues immediately. Most importantly, your eight hours of sleep is important.

Create A "Me Time"

It's not selfish to dedicate a little time to a hobby; do something that you enjoy for yourself. Having me time will reenergize you and give you the energy to chase your goals.

Build Healthy Friendships

As mentioned in a previous chapter, you can't walk alone. Forming strong and healthy relationships will aid you to achieve your goals faster than when alone. Seek out for friends who accept you for who you are. Furthermore, build a friendship with those that model the qualities you desire.

Chapter 11:
Never Ring the Bell

There are moments in our lives where we feel all hope has been dashed out, and possibly, taking the next leap may be difficult. This situation happens a lot, and it can be very dramatic and traumatizing, I must confess. But it is necessary to have it in mind that many persons pass through this phase as they mature; so, luckily, you are not in this boat alone. Everyone at some point in their lives has felt the need to quit and run away even without trying. But did you know that many successful persons we know today, repeatedly tried without giving up? Yes, they never gave up. You need to see it as a motivating force. So, whenever this negative feeling of staying down creeps into you, brush it up, keep moving, and never quench the zeal to persevere. You know, it would sound unrealistic if a person told you they'd never had a challenge while growing up; of course, it's never been heard of and as far as I am concerned, it is unbelievable.

Nobody has it all and life isn't a bed of roses; even the kids born with the silver spoons can attest to that fact. So, if anyone ever told you there won't be struggles, challenges, setbacks, and failures, the person lied to you, and of course, you need to wake up from such dreams.

Furthermore, you need to know that the world is messed up and sincerely, everyone is struggling to make a life out of it. The topsy-turvy of life is a constant factor, and our fears and challenges are a sure thing. Also, facing short and long-term failures are all a part of growing up. But you would agree with me on this note that all situations in life have their seasons. Some may be unpleasant, yes, and others may be good. But, in as much as we have these feelings of fear and doubt, it is paramount to know that unpleasant situations are not a permanent phase in life. Although to some people, it might feel that their share of bad moments is much more than others, this in no way should deplete ones motivating force. And, it should for no reason turn you into a weakling or make you quit even before trying. It is just a phase, and you need to persevere whatever the cost may be.

So, What Is Perseverance?

Perseverance sometimes may be referred to as determination, courage, fearlessness, and endurance. Furthermore, it also can mean steady persistence in carrying out an action, purpose, or a dream despite the challenge faced. Having defined this term, I will give an example of someone who persevered.

You Owe Yourself A Breakthrough

Curt and Lewis were one of those kids in high school who knew what they wanted in life. Dreamers and writers—those were the right words to qualify them with. Their raw talents for writing were second to none. Curt's parents got him a tutor to polish him more with his writing skills. Lewis, on the other hand, had no one to put him through but himself and his mom. They both, in their ways, mastered the act since it was what they enjoyed doing. Most of their free times was devoted to writing and they improved each time they took the pen.

Interestingly, their family and friends were impressed with their growth because their stories were good enough to be published; but it never crossed their minds that someday, they could make a living from it. More so, the writing was what they did for leisure; it was never a chore. So, imagining their leisurely craft being published as a book was less thought to envisage. But a few years later, after graduation, they knew for a fact that their act could grow more than a hobby. So, they took a bold step and mailed some of their stories to a magazine, hoping it would be published. But sadly, it was rejected.

Unlike their friends and families who enjoyed reading their work, the magazine decided that their stories were crap and weren't worth reading. And so, they felt incapable and thought they could not write anymore. But to everyone's surprise, they wrote yet another story; and for the second time, it was rejected. These rejections consistently happened with three more attempts. You would agree it was spirit breaking, and of a truth it was. Who knows? Maybe you would also agree with the publishers that their first work was tacky. But then, one would also ask, "what happened to the rest of the stories they submitted?"

How To

Were they not good enough to be published? Was it just a coincidence that all their works were rejected? Or maybe it was fate dealing with them? Sincerely, neither was the case here. The whole incident made Curt wallow in self-pity, and he concluded "it was fate" and probably, writing, after all, wasn't his gift; so, he stopped after the fifth time. But luckily for Lewis, his mindset was way different and he, however, continued writing and sent his new stories even upon rejection.

Interestingly, after a few years, he got a call from the same magazine, and that, I would say, was a breakthrough call. Of a truth, there were times Lewis almost gave up because it took almost forever to get the attention of the publisher. More so, there were moments he also thought it was best to quit. Nonetheless, he encouraged himself and persevered all through the difficult periods.

So, Be the Judge

Who amongst these two got better with writing? Who amongst them was given a chance? Who was ready to leap? Who gave up and who persevered? Lewis? Curt? Maybe I know your answers already.

Lewis got a response after years of perseverance and today, he has over a hundred books to his name. The truth in life is that people who keep trying, people who never quit, those who persevere at all odds, those who have vowed to never stay down no matter the rejection, no matter the number of times they are walked over, no matter the number of times they get a no; those I tell you, are the people who are likely to keep getting better opportunities in life. For a fact, the only obstacle to your breakthrough is you. You don't have to blame anyone else for the choices you make in life. No one promises a smooth ride; it is going to be a rough one, but no matter the number of times the vehicle stops, you need to take up the steering and zoom off.

Stop Making Excuses for Yourself

Excuses have become a syndrome to our daily lives; because the human brain is wired in such a way to give up easily, many people have become caught up in its web. Some individuals unconsciously see excuses as a trophy to be won and in fact, you'd find out that before any ideas are suggested to them, they are already giving a thousand and one reasons as to why it will not be successful. And the truth is, if maximum caution is not taken to this effect, these individuals will constantly see reasons to still be buried in their mess. Well, it is necessary to know that no blames are intended to these people. I have been among this category of persons, so I have a fair idea as to what extent the void may create. I often saw reasons why I couldn't continue with a pursuit anymore, and I gave excuses that were worthless. Most of the time, I drowned in my self-pity and blamed everyone else for it; it became a little difficult to break free. The truth is, everyone faces setbacks, but some have a way of turning it into a driving force. And others at the other hand see it as a point to stop; this attitude I will say would only lead to self-destruct. So, in as much as you want to be a success story to another person, it is necessary to pick up the broken pieces and save yourself from the dangers of staying down.

Decide and Achieve What You Want

Indisputably, no meaningful achievements have been accomplished without the topsy-turvy of life. It would shock you to know that most successful persons on Earth have passed through challenges that can ordinarily make a person question existence. And the truth is, we look up to these folks and want to achieve their successes. But we feel very reluctant to make the sacrifices they made; because everybody wants the easy bailout. If you care to know, nothing in life comes at the snap of a finger, you will, of course, pay some prices to achieve this feat. The price in this case is perseverance. More so, deciding the things you want to achieve in life will come with a lot of hiccups, but firstly, you need to take control of your happiness. This feeling has a way of making some persons achieve their daily goals. So, if you want to keep your decision and achievements alive, then you need to own it and do what makes you happy.

Prepare for Challenges

Well, setting new goals and starting them can be quite intriguing; actually, anyone can do it if they put their minds to it. But also, you would concur with me that apart from having ideas for a new project, there are other difficult tasks associated with achieving one's goal. Having great ideas is not a bad thing after all, but you need to be acquainted with the possibilities of failing. One needs to know and expect that challenges will surface; this knowledge of possible challenge would make you prepare ahead of time because no great achievement was ever accomplished without setbacks. So, if you don't want to quit after a few steps, then you need to be cautious of the fact that challenges are inevitable. For example, if I need to open an online store, I must make inquiries first about it. Of course, it would be unwise to jump into it because I have a dream of being an online store owner. So, to get me on track, I must seek enough counsel from established online store owners in order not to ruin the business even before it kicks off. More so, there would need to ask the question about challenges faced by online store owners; and these may include questions relating from poor website traffic, lack of capital, loyal customers, tax, inventory management, too many more. This, as you can see, would prepare me for any future occurrence and make me have an idea about subsequent challenge or failure in this line of work. So, in the long run, if I have the zeal to quit, I would strive to never give up.

Take the Bold Step

Fear is a factor on its own that negatively affects one's success. It makes a person frozen in their own time and for this reason, leads to unnecessary procrastination. You would be baffled to know that some dreams and great ideas have been sent to the abyss because of fear. But for a fact, I'd prefer I died to try rather than allow fear to prevent me from trying and achieving my goals. And of course, I've never in my lifetime heard about a person who was celebrated for not trying.

How To

So, if you want to succeed in life, ask yourself tough questions as to why you cannot decide on a course of action. Asking these questions will not in any way harm you; the only thing it will do is help you filter your thoughts. So, peradventure the benefit of taking the first step outweighs your fears, then you are on the right part to the success, and in fact, you are good to go. In a nutshell, my advice to you is to never quit before trying, because you can only persevere when you take the first step.

Maintaining Focus

There are no shortcuts to great achievements. No successful person in history has taken the easy route; it is always a long path to success. Never giving up no matter the challenge has always been the way to go. And for a fact, if you need to maintain focus with a career or chosen field, you need to look past obstacles. You cannot persevere—much less be successful—if you forget the reason why you started. Of a truth, it is never an easy task. But it is necessary to occasionally look at the price tag as you accomplish your life goals. More so, maintaining focus would help you overcome any negative thought that would stand as a hindrance to achieving your set goals.

A befitting example would be that of a runner who sees the finish line and decides to get there. Truthfully, there may be side distractions to him finishing first; because our brains are finely attuned to see extreme agitation that diverts our attention. But you see, the price tag would be the only driving force that would push him to finish that race.

Furthermore, as an entrepreneur, maintaining focus can sometimes seem almost impossible because of some things you need to do; such as a continuous track of phone calls, emails, clients, and employees. So, in situations like this, having keen knowledge of your brains limitations and pushing past these limitations can enhance your focus and boost your productivity. Also, multitasking has been said to be another factor to losing focus. In as much as it is an important skill to our everyday lives, it also has a negative side which consequently reduces our intelligence to a certain percentage; dropping our brain power. Some research has shown that when we multitask, we get emotionally tensed up and make mistakes because of some we need to do all at once. So basically, the aim is not to constantly focus but to also have a bit of free time when multitasking. But all in all, when having this free time, make sure you don't drown excessively in it because it might shift your gaze. So, my advice to you; put on a positive mindset all the time and never lose focus.

Seek Help and Support

No one can achieve success alone. I am often amazed when people say they are self-made; it gives me chills because I know for sure that it is practically impossible. Sometimes, you may decide not to involve some persons to your plans, because of some reasons best known to you. But have it in mind, too, that some certain set of individuals—strangers, colleagues, chauffeur or even a cook—has a role to play either intentionally or unintentionally. So, for sure, everyone in their little ways contribute to a success story. Also, it is paramount to know that seeking help sometimes can be difficult; particularly when a person is in a state of dilemma.

Nonetheless, always solicit for support or help when you are in dire need of it. Furthermore, do not hesitate to dissociate yourself from people who are addicted to having a pessimistic view about success; because they will eventually leave you in the dark. One thing for sure is important here: when seeking help, get it from the right folks, get it from people who are more experienced in your chosen field of interest, and finally, get support from people who are happy to see you succeed—these are the people who will instigate that perseverance fervor into you.

Review Your Achievements and Failure

Before I go in-depth with this piece, I will like to give a quick description of what review means. According to several definitions, a review can be described as a critical evaluation or inspection for text or report; in other words, review may be referred to as an analysis of a piece of work. Interestingly, this word has saved many businesses, persons, and firms from the edge of collapse. You know, quite a few persons make great plans but most times, when these great ideas don't break through, then their world tends to be on a landslide; this is one of the reasons why a lot of individuals stay down after the first try. Well, it will interest you to know that one of the keys to being successful in life is reviewing and reevaluating set goals. So, if peradventure an idea fails, the best resurrection you could offer it is to review the patterns or steps you took at the first instance, and then try a different one. Furthermore, as failure is reviewed, success, on the other hand, needs to be reevaluated; because it would be a blow if after succeeding, one begins to retrogress. So, to achieve more in life, you need to constantly review, reevaluate, and most especially persevere through it all because your starting point to success is way beyond the sky.

Chapter 12:
Final Note

Congratulations on reading to the end. It was an eventful journey for both of us. For me, it's the fulfillment of a long-term goal: to write a book on money and success habits. On the other hand, it's a guideline for achieving your dreams, and an affirmation of your positive and negative actions in the journey of life. Yes, we have practically touched every aspect you need to know to tap into your inner giant. However, one part was omitted. Perhaps, I saved the best part for the last. Well, it's up to you, my dear reader, to decide if this part is truly the icing on the cake.

Your Goals Are Everything!
Yes, this is one part that was omitted. Although we explored this concept in different chapters, we only talked about specific areas that applied to the subject at hand. This time get ready to have an undiluted front seat to the word that has made giants out of small men. Before we delve into this amazing concept, I want you to read and follow this chapter actively rather than passively. Munch on it and incorporate it into everything you do. I'll advise you to read it repeatedly.

Jeremy Napier

Goals are everything. Every achievement is a testament to the fulfillment of a goal. Look around you at the buildings, mega-corporations, and the little shops that dot your street; they are all the product of someone or a group of people's goals. Let's make it simple: look at your TV set, your smartphones, and laptops. All these objects were once ideas or dreams in someone's head. A century ago, no one would have believed that these objects would exist. There's more: the solution to some of our current challenges lies in someone's imagination right now. Some people's goals are just to pay their bills, to survive and have enough to get by, while some set giant goals to change their status quo. You should know that irrespective of your goals, you will never get to your destination if you don't take the step. Remember, all goal settings are followed by a plan formation and massive and consistent actions toward its fulfillment.

What's Stopping You from Setting Goals

We all have the power to act on your goals. The fact that we haven't been able to access the power is because we've failed to set goals that inspire us. So, what stops us from having a clear list of goals to improve mentally physically, financial, and emotionally? Is it the fear of disappointment? Some stopped setting goals because they failed to achieve them in the past, and they can't get over the fear of disappointment. On the other hand, some set goals and attach their happiness to goals that might be beyond their control. These set of folks may lack the flexibility to notice better and more worthy goals around them while moving in the direction of their goals.

We fail to realize that the process of setting goals works like our eyesight; the closer we get to our destination, the more clarity we gain, not only on the goal itself but on the details around the goal. Perhaps, you might prefer one of those other possibilities. As you read on, you will discover that pursuing your goals brings you closer to your life's true purpose.

The strength to chase your goals may come from life's many disappointments or the stark realization that life is passing you by. For others, inspiration is a source of motivation. Irrespective of your source of motivation, I would like to introduce you to the key to achieve your goals.

The Key to Achieving Your Goals

When you take the step to achieve your goals, you've acknowledged the desire that we all have for constant improvement. There's a power in being dissatisfied with your current situation. There's a power in the tension of temporary discomfort. This strength will help you to push on through the pain and the discouragement. To achieve your goals, you need a certain level of discomfort to motivate you to push forward and increase the quality of your life and those around you. Many people try to shy away from discomfort or pressure, yet it is the absence of pressure creates a sense of boredom and lackluster character toward life. Truthfully, we feel excited or alive when we feel pressure of discomfort within us. However, this is different when we are overwhelmed by pressure or tension. There's a difference between being overwhelmed by stress and being the master of stress. Therefore, become the master of stress and use it to move you in the direction you desire. More so, you could put yourself under stress by enlisting the help of those you respect to accomplish your goals. Simply announce before these people that you would do everything in your power to pursue your goals. So, whenever you want to quit, you would remember your public announcement and push on.

Live Life to The Fullest!

It's sad to see some putting off joy and happiness in the pursuit of their goals. They believe that they will truly become happy and enjoy life to the fullest once they achieve something. Well, here's the truth: you stand to achieve more when you are happy and joyful. Although goals give us a sense of direction, we must constantly strive to live each day to the fullest, with no compromise. Do not measure your failure or success in life by the accomplishment of each specific goal you set. Remember that the direction you are heading to is more important not the specific goals. Sometimes, you may never get to accomplish that goal. However, the fact that you are in the right direction is an advantage since you would meet other goals to achieve.

Create Your Future

How To

Here's a question for you: what would you do if you knew you couldn't fail? As the thought runs in your mind, I want you to write it down. Don't bother with the specifics of the goals. Just write, "Picturesque recreation center, Bahamas" or "Dream House, Big Garden, Beverly Hills."—you will fill in the details later. Now, I want you to believe and have the assurance that you can attain these goals. Divide your goals into personal development goals, adventure goals, contribution goals, and business/career goals.

Your Personal Development Goals

These goals are centered on your physical, mental, and social development. In this section, write everything you would like to improve in your life about your personal growth. You might want to learn a new language or read 52 books in a year. In terms of emotional growth, ask yourself the self-inflicting patterns you want to break or the toxic relationship you want to quit. Perhaps, you want to learn how to feel compassion for those you abhor. Mind you, the secret is to keep on writing these goals without stopping. Write to them as they come to mind. It could be a short-term goal that you can accomplish within a week or month. Alternatively, it might be a long-term goal that takes years to achieve.

Once you've written down your goals, take a minute to add a timeline to each goal. Hold on! Don't get scared about how you are going to accomplish these goals—it's not important. Rather, I want you to set a timeframe for each goal. This will condition the subconscious and conscious to make those changes goals possible.

Choose your most important goal. Choose a goal that would give you much excitement and fulfillment if you achieved it within a year. Now take a few minutes to write a compelling paragraph on why you are committed to achieving this goal. Write down what you will gain by achieving it. Ask yourself, "What would I miss out on if I don't achieve it?" These are the reasons and questions you need to consider when you feel like giving up on your goals. Make these your driving force and you will achieve beyond your imagination.

Career Goals

In this section, write down your goals for your career, business, and financial status. Set a standard you want to meet. Once again, take a few minutes to pen out your goals. Just keep writing as it comes to mind. These goals could revolve around why you would like to become the leader in your company, your net worth at a certain age, your retirement age, and so many more you deem as important. Now, follow the same strategy as your personal development goals.

Achieving Your Goal Is Not the End

Most people have the misconception that achieving our goals is the end. We fail to realize that by pursuing our goals, we create a ripple effect that affects our environment. For instance, a businessman sets out with the goal to build a business and earn a profit. In the course of earning money, he/she creates jobs for people. More so, these folks, in turn, provided a livelihood for their family. Furthermore, the kids contribute by becoming doctors, lawyers or any professional and nonprofessional job. No doubt, it's an unending circle.

See your goals as a transport medium to a destination, and not as the end of the journey itself. Remember, your goals are the tool to help steer you in the right direction. More so, achieving your goals will never make you happy in the long-term. Rather, it's who you become that gives you long-term happiness.

Here's one more secret for you: never delay your goals. Once you write it, take the step immediately. You might not have the required motivation to tackle the task again. Start while it's still fresh in your mind. With this in-depth analysis, you can comfortably reach your goals.

If you find this book helpful in anyway a review to support my endeavors is much appreciated.

Jeremy Napier

How To

www.ingramcontent.com/pod-product-compliance
Lightning Source LLC
Chambersburg PA
CBHW020402080526
44584CB00014B/1136